WEB

DEVELOPMENT

WEB DEVELOPMENT
FOR BEGINNERS IN HTML

Andy Vickler

Table of Contents

Introduction

HTML is the primary web language, not surprising given that it is used to write most web pages – learning it well and truly puts you on the right path to creating some pretty amazing websites. What you will learn here is what makes up an HTML document, all the different elements involved, and how to use them.

In each chapter, you will find simple code examples showing you how each element works, along with simple explanations on how it all works. At the end of the book, there is one last chapter that runs you through building a simple web page from start to finish using HTML.

In 1989, Tim Berners-Lee invented something that would change the world as we knew it and continues to change the world today. That invention was the World Wide Web, and back then, he didn't have access to fancy programming languages like JavaScript and CSS; all he had was HTML.

Over the last 30 years or so, HTML has changed, almost beyond recognition but not quite. It now has well over 120 tags, significantly more than the 18 it started with and is still the central, most important part of any web page. It is, in short, the web's foundational technology.

If your website has its basis in good HTML, you will have a fast-loading site. Browsers will render HTML incrementally, meaning the user sees a partly rendered page while the browser waits for the rest of the files to come from the server.

Modern development techniques, fashionable ones like React, need the user to be sent a lot of JavaScript, which, once downloaded, must be parsed by the user's device and executed. And all that has to happen before the web page can be constructed. If your network is slow, or your device is low-powered or low-end, the load time can be excruciatingly slow and drains the device battery.

If your site is based on decent HTML, it will be robust. While scripts and styles may take longer to load, the content will always be available, and HTML is not only backward compatible, but it is also future-proof – it will always work.

Who Writes HTML Anymore?

I often hear people saying that there's no need to learn HTML these days because let's face it, who writes it by hand anymore? Sure, there is a lot of truth to this – WordPress powers just over 35% of the web these days. This uses templates to assemble web pages, and different themes can be applied to them. Drupal and Joomla work in much the same way. At the same time, other developers use React and other similar frameworks that simply put together a series of components that have already been written.

But let's face it – those components and templates still need to be written. And those developers who use React or WordPress still need some HTML knowledge. Otherwise, they cannot evaluate how good the components and templates are before they use them.

And that is why I produced this guide, so that you know how to produce a web page in good old-fashioned HTML and not have to worry about how good, or otherwise, someone else's work is.

Chapter 1

What is HTML?

HTML stands for **HyperText Markup Language**, and it is the language used to create web applications and web pages. So, what does it all mean?

- **HyperText** – this means nothing more than "text in text." Any text that contains a link is known as one of two things – a hyperlink or hypertext. If you click on one of these links, a new web page will open. It is used to link web pages together, ensuring users can easily jump between them.

- **Markup Language** – markup languages are computer languages used for applying formatting and layout to a document. These languages ensure that text is more dynamic and interactive and can be used to turn text into links, tables, images, and more.

- **Web Pages** – web pages are documents that are usually written in HTML, and a web browser is then used to translate them. We access and identify these web pages using URLs, the address where the web page is located on the internet, and they can be dynamic or static. The only language that can be used to create static web pages is HTML.

All of that means that the HTML language is used to create nice-looking web pages by using styling and showing them on a web page in a nice format. HTML documents comprise multiple tags, each tag having different content.

Let's put all this into context by looking at a simple HTML example:

```
<!DOCTYPE>
<html>
<head>
<title>Web page title</title>
</head>
<body>
<h1>Your first heading goes here</h1>
<p>Your first paragraph goes here</p>
</body>
</html>
```

Running this would display this on your screen:

Your first heading goes here

Your first paragraph goes here

Let's break this example down into its components:

- **<!DOCTYPE>** - this defines the type of document or tells the browser what HTML version is being used.

- **<html >** this tells the browser an HTML document is being used. Any text in between this tag is describing the document. In other words, it is a container for every other HTML element, with the exception of <!DOCTYPE>.

- **<head>** - this is the first element in the <html> tag and it contains details about the document, i.e., the metadata. Before the body tag is opened, the <head> tag must be closed.

- **<title>** - the name says it all – this tag adds the title of the web page, the title seen at the top of the window displayed in the browser. It must be inside the head tag, and it should be immediately closed.

- **<body>** - this is where the web page content goes, the content the end-user sees. It is the main HTML document content.

- **<h1>** - any text in this tag is describing the web page's first-level heading.

- **<p>** - the text in this tag is describing the web page's paragraph text.

All of this will become clearer as you work through this book.

A Brief HTML History

Tim Berners-Lee was a physicist in the late 80s, contracted to work at CERN. While he was there, he proposed a system for researchers and, in 1989, he sent a memo containing a hypertext system based on the internet.

He has earned the moniker of "the father of HTML." In 1991, he produced a document called "HTML Tags," the very first HTML description.

HTML Versions

Since HTML was first invented, several versions have been released:

- **HTML 1.0** – Released in 1991, this was the first version of HTML and was very basic.

- **HTML 2.0** - The next version was released in 1995 and became the website design standard. It provided support for extra features, including form elements, like option buttons, text boxes, etc., and form based file uploads.

- **HTML 3.2** - W3C released this version early in 1997 and brought support for table creation and more support for new options in form elements. It could also support web pages containing complex math equations. In January 1997, it became the browser standard and, today, it is still supported by most browsers in a practical form.

- **HTML 4.01** – The next HTML version came about in December 1999 and proved incredibly stable – it still is today. It is the official standard we work with currently and provides support for CSS (stylesheets) and scripting ability for different multimedia elements.

- **HTML5** - HTML5 is the latest version and was first announced in January 2008. Two large foundations are involved in HTML 5 development – World Wide Web Consortium (W3C) and Web Hypertext Application Technology Working Group (WHATWG) and, today, it is still being developed.

HTML Features

So, why use HTML? Why not use one of the newer languages, such as JavaScript? Apart from the fact that HTML supports JavaScript and CSS, it offers users all these features:

1. It is one of the easiest languages to understand and modify

2. Making effective presentations with HTML is easy because it offers tons of formatting tags

3. Because it is a markup language, it gives users a flexible way of designing web pages with text

4. It allows users to add links on web pages using the anchor tag, thus enhancing the user's browsing interest

5. It is not dependent on any specific platform and can be displayed on Windows Linux, Mac, and all others

6. It allows programmers to easily add sound, videos, and graphics to their pages, ensuring they are more interactive and attractive

7. It is not case sensitive like other languages, so tags can be used both lower and uppercase. However, the recommendation is to use lower-case for readability and consistency

HTML Text Editors

Because HTML files are text files, they need to be created in a text editor. A text editor is a program that allows you to edit the text to create your web page. There are many different ones available to download, but beginners are urged to use Notepad if they use Windows or TextEdit if they use macOS. Once you have learned the basics, you can move onto other professional editors, such as Vim, Sublime Text, Notepad++, and so on.

Using Notepad or TextEdit

Step One – Opening Notepad (Windows)

If you use Windows 8 or above:

- Open your Start Screen

- Type in Notepad

If you use Windows 7 or lower:

- Open Start

- Click on Programs>Accessories

- Click on Notepad

Opening TextEdit (macOS)

- Open Finder

- Click on Applications>TextEdit

You will also need to change a few preferences, so the application saves your files properly:

- Open Preferences

- Click on Format>Plain Text

- Click on Open and Save

- Check the box beside "Display HTML files as HTML code instead of formatted text."

- Open a document to put your code in

Step Two – Writing Your HTML Code

Write the following code into your Notepad or Text Edit document. You can type it in by hand or copy and paste it:

```
<!DOCTYPE html>
<html>
<body>

<h1>My First Heading</h1>

<p>My first paragraph.</p>

</body>
</html>
```

Step Three – Save the Page

- To save the file, click on File>Save As

- Call the file "index.htm" and ensure the encoding is set as the preferred HTML encoding, UTF-8.

There are two file extensions you can use - .htm or .html. It doesn't matter which as there is no difference between them.

Step Four – View it in Your Browser

- Open index.htm in your browser by double-clicking the file. Alternatively, you can right-click on the file and click on Open With

You should see, on your screen, a web page showing your desktop location as the URL and the following on the screen:

My First Heading

My First Paragraph

Here's another simple HTML example that you can try out:

```
<!DOCTYPE html>
<html>
<head>
<title>Page Title</title>
</head>
<body>

<h1>This is a Heading</h1>
<p>This is a paragraph.</p>

</body>
</html>
```

HTML Basic Examples

To finish this chapter, we'll look at some basic examples. These will include tags you will come across throughout this book; don't worry if you don't understand them yet. You will do by the end.

HTML Documents

- Every HTML document must have a declaration stating the document type - <!DOCTYPE html>

- The document must start with <html> and end up with </body>

- The part of the HTML document visible to users goes between the <body> and </body> tags

Here's an example:

```
<!DOCTYPE html>
<html>
<body>

<h1>My First Heading</h1>
<p>My first paragraph.</p>

</body>
</html>
```

<!DOCTYPE> Declaration

- This indicates the type of document, ensuring web browsers can correctly display web pages

- It should only be in the text once, right at the start of the page, and before any tags

- The declaration is case-insensitive

The HTML5 declaration is:

```
<!DOCTYPE html>
```

HTML Headings

There are several tags used to define HTML headings - <h1>, <h2>, <h3>, <h4>, <h5>, and <h6>. <H1> is the most important and <h6> is the least important.

```
<h1>This is heading 1</h1>
<h2>This is heading 2</h2>
<h3>This is heading 3</h3>
```

HTML Paragraphs

The <p> tag is used to define HTML paragraphs:

```
<p>This is a paragraph.</p>
<p>This is another paragraph.</p>
```

HTML Links

The <a> tag is used to define HTML links:

```
<a href="https://www.wikipedia.com">This is
a link</a>
```

The href attribute is used to specify the link's destination. We'll talk about attributes in the next chapter but, right now, all you need to know is that they are used for providing more information about elements.

HTML Images

The <img> tag is used to define HTML images, and the attributes are src (source file), alt (alternative text), height, and width.

```
<img src="wikipedia.jpg" alt="Wikipedia.com"
width="104" height="142">
```

How to View HTML Sources

How many times have you looked at a web page and wondered how it was created? On any HTML web page, all you need to do is right-click the page. In Chrome browser, click on View Page Source or, in Edge, click on View Source. It's much the same in other browsers. A window opens, showing you the page's source code.

How to Inspect HTML Elements

Simply right-click a blank area or an element and click on Inspect Element or Inspect. This will show you both the HTML and CSS parts of the element, and you can also use the Styles or Elements panel to edit the HTML.

In the next chapter, we'll look at the building blocks that go into HTML.

Chapter 2

HTML Building Blocks

L et's dive straight into this – an HTML document is made up of building blocks. The basic ones are:

- **Tags** – HTML tags are used to surround content and give it some meaning. All tags are surrounded by <>

- **Attributes** – HTML attributes provide additional details about elements, and the start tag is used to apply them. All attributes have two fields, name and value.

We'll also be discussing elements in this chapter.

Syntax

```
<tag name attribute_name= "
attr_value">content</tag name>
```

HTML elements are individual HTML file components and anything written in a tag is known as an element.

ELEMENT

START TAG	CONTENT	END TAG
<p class ="gfg">	This is my webpage	</p>

Attribute name — Attribute value

Attribute

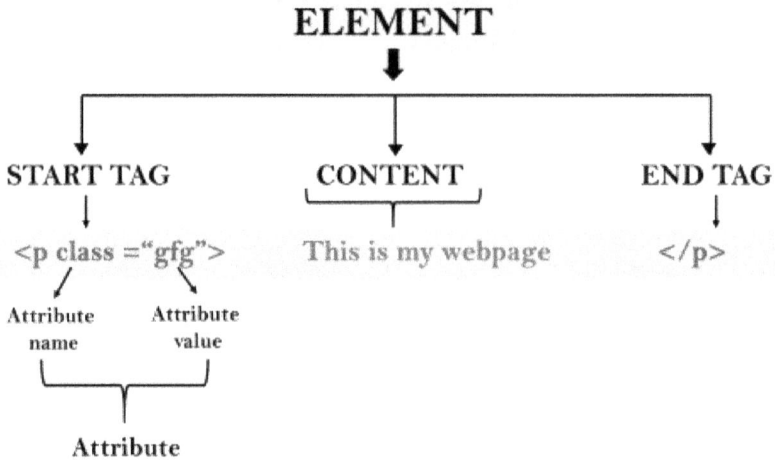

Here's an example:

```
<!DOCTYPE html>
<html>
  <head>
    <title>The basic HTML building blocks
</title>
  </head>
    <body>
        <h2>The building blocks</h2>
        <p>This is a paragraph tag</p>
        <p style="color: red">The style is an
attribute of the paragraph tag</p>
        <span>The element contains a tag, an
attribute and content</span>
    </body>
</html>
```

The output of this is:

The building blocks

The style is an attribute of the paragraph tag

The element contains a tag, an attribute, and content

HTML Table Tags

The table tags you are likely to use are:

- Table
- tr
- td
- th
- tbody
- thead
- tfoot
- col
- colgroup
- caption

HTML Form Tags

The form tags are:

- form
- input

- textarea

- select

- option

- optgroup

- button

- label

- fieldset

- legend

HTML Scripting Tags

There are two scripting tags:

- script

- noscript

HTML Tags

You can think of HTML tags as being similar to keywords. They define the way a browser formats content and displays it. By using tags, web browsers can distinguish between HTML and simple content. There are three primary parts to a tag – the opening tag, the content, and the closing tag. However, some HTML tags are unclosed.

When a browser reads an HTML document, it is read from the top down and from left to right – the same way you would read the pages in a book. HTML documents are created by HTML tags and render the properties – every tag has its own properties.

HTML files need essential tags to allow the browser to tell the difference between HTML and simple text. As per the requirements of your code, you can use as many tags as you need.

- Every HTML tag should be enclosed between brackets - <>

- All HTML tags do different things

- If an open tag is used (<tag>) then, in most cases, there must be a close tag (</tag>.)

Syntax

```
<tag> content </tag>
```

HTML Tag Examples

All HTML tags should be written in lowercase letters. These are the most basic tags:

- <p> Paragraph Tag </p>

- <h2> Heading Tag </h2>

- <b> **Bold Tag** </b>

- <i> *Italic Tag* </i>

- <u> Underline Tag</u>

Unclosed HTML Tags

Not all HTML tags need to be closed. For example:

- **
 Tag** – br is a break line tag, used to break code lines

- **<hr> Tag** – hr is a horizontal rule tag, used for inserting a line across the page

HTML Meta Tags

The html meta tags are:

- DOCTYPE

- title

- link

- meta

- style

HTML Text Tags

The commonly used text tags are:

- <p>

- <h1>

- <h2>

- <h3>

- <h4>

- <h5>

- `<h6>`
- `<strong>`
- `<em>`
- `<abbr>`
- `<acronym>`
- `<address>`
- `<bdo>`
- `<blockquote>`
- `<cite>`
- `<q>`
- `<code>`
- `<ins>`
- `<del>`
- `<dfn>`
- `<kbd>`
- `<pre>`
- `<samp>`
- `<var>`
- `<br>`

HTML Link Tags

There are two link tags:

- <a>

- <base>

HTML Object and Image Tags

The main object and image tags are:

- <img>

- <area>

- <map>

- <param>

- <object>

HTML List Tags

The primary list tags are:

- <ul>

- <ol>

- <li>

- <dl>

- <dt>

- <dd>

HTML Tags List

The following list is all the HTML tags, in alphabetical order so you can find what you want easily, and each with a description. Those with an asterisk (*) are the recently added elements to HTML5:

TAG	DESCRIPTION
<!-- -->	This is used when you need a comment applied in an HTML document
<!DOCTYPE>	This is used to specify the HTML version
<a>	This is the anchor tag and is used to create links or hyperlinks
<abbr>	This is used for creating abbreviations for longer words or phrases
<acronym>	This defines acronyms for specified words – HTML5 does NOT support this
<address>	This defines the contact info for the HTML article author
<applet>	This defines embedded Java applets – HTML5 does NOT support this
<area>	This defines an image map's area

\<article\>*	This defined content that is self-contained
\<aside\>*	This defines content separate from the primary content – usually shown as a sidebar
\<audio\>*	This is used when you want sound embedded in an HTML document
\<b\>	This is used when you want the text in bold
\<base\>	This is used to define the base URL for all other URLs (relative) in the same document
\<basefont\>	This is used for setting the default font, color, and size for all the document elements
\<bdi\>*	This tag isolates a specified section of text to be formatted differently from the text surrounding it
\<bdo\>	This tag overrides the text's current direction
\<big\>	This makes the size of the font one larger than the content surrounding it – HTML5 does NOT support this

\<blockquote\>	This defines any content taken from a different source
\<body\>	This defines the HTML document's body section
\<br\>	This applies one line break
\<button\>	This represents clickable buttons
\<canvas\>*	This tag is used for providing a web document with a graphics space
\<caption\>	This is used for defining captions for tables
\<center\>	This is used to center align content HTML5 does NOT support this
\<cite\>	This is used to define a title for a book, website, or other work
\<code\>	This is used for displaying a specified section of code from the HTML document
\<col\>	This defines columns in a table that represents the common column properties and is used with the element called \<colgroup\>

<colgroup>	This is used for defining column groups in tables
<data>*	This is used for linking content using a machine-readable translation
<datalist>*	This is used to provide an input option of a predefined list
<dd>	This provides a description or a definition of a description list term
<del>	This defines text that was deleted
<details>*	This defines extra information that can be viewed or hidden by a user
<dfn>	This indicates a term defined in a phrase or sentence
<dialog>*	This defines interactive components such as a dialog box
<dir>	This is used as a type of container to hold a directory list of all files – HTML5 does NOT support this
<div>	This defines sections or divisions in a document
<dl>	This defines description lists
<dt>	This defines a description list term

\<em\>	This emphasizes content within the element
\<embed\>*	This is an embedded container to hold external media, applications, files, etc.
\<fieldset\>	This groups labels or elements that are related in a web form
\<figcaption\>*	This adds explanations or captions for \<figure\>
\<figure\>*	This defines self-contained content
\<font\>	This defines the face, font, size, and color of the content – HTML5 does NOT support this
\<footer\>*	This defines the web page's footer
\<form\>	This defines an HTML form
\<frame\>	This defines a specified part of the page which may have another HTML file in it – HTML5 does NOT support this
\<frameset\>	This fines a Frames group – HTML5 does NOT support this
\<h1\> to \<h6\>	This defines the different heading levels in a document

<head>	This defines the HTML document's head section
<header>*	This defines a web page's header
<hr>	This applies thematic breaks between the elements at paragraph-level
<html>	This represents the HTML document's root
<i>	This uses a different voice to represent text
<iframe>	This defines inline frames used for embedding other content
<img>	This is used for inserting images in HTML documents
<input>	This defines an HTML form's input fields
<ins>	This represents text inserted in a document
<isindex>	This displays search strings for the current document – HTML5 does NOT support it
<kbd>	This defines keyboard input
<label>	This defines a form's input field label

\<legend\>	This defines a caption for \<fieldset\> content
\<li\>	This is used for representing list items
\<link\>	This is used for representing relationships between external resources and current documents
\<main\>*	This is used to represent an HTML documents main content
\<map\>	This defines image maps with active areas
\<mark\>*	This is used to represent highlighted text
\<marquee\>	This is used for inserting scrolling text or images, vertically or horizontally – HTML5 does NOT support this
\<menu\>	This is used to create menu lists containing commands
\<meta\>	This defines an HTML document's metadata
\<meter\>*	This is used to define a scalar measurement with a fractional value or a known range

\<nav\>*	This is used for representing page sections representing navigation links
\<noframes\>	This provides alternative content to show in browsers where the \<fame\> element is not supported – HTML5 does NOT support this
\<noscript\>	This provides alternate content where a browser does not support the script type
\<object\>	This is used for embedding objects in HTML files
\<ol\>	This is used to define ordered item lists
\<optgroup\>	This is used to group a drop-down list's options
\<option\>	This is used to define a drop-down list's items or options
\<output\>*	This is used as a container and shows a calculation's result
\<p\>	This is used to represent HTML document paragraphs
\<param\>	This is used to define an \<object\> element's parameters

\<picture\>*	This is used to define multiple source elements and an image element
\<pre\>	This is used for defining an HTML document's pre-formatted text
\<progress\>*	This is used for defining a task's progress in an HTML document
\<q\>	This is used for defining short inline quotations
\<rp\>*	This is used to define alternate content where ruby annotations are not supported by a browser
\<rt\>	This is used for defining ruby annotation pronunciations and explanations
\<ruby\>	This is used for representing ruby annotations
\<s\>	This is used for rendering incorrect or irrelevant text
\<samp\>	This is used for representing a computer program's sample outputs
\<script\>	This is used for declaring an HTML document's JavaScript

\<section\>*	This is used for defining a document's generic sections
\<select\>	This is used for representing a control which, in turn, provides an options menu
\<small\>	This is used for decreasing font by one size smaller than the base font size for the document
\<source\>\>*	This is used for defining multiple recourse for media elements, such as \<audio\>, \<video\> and \<picture\> elements
\<span\>	This is used for inline grouping and styling
\<strike\>	This renders a strike-through specified text – HTML5 does NOT support this
\<strong\>	This is used when you want important text defined
\<style\>	This is used for holding an HTML document's style information
\<sub\>	This is used for defining text you want to be displayed as a subscript text

\<summary\>*	This is used for defining summaries for use with the \<details\> tag
\<sup\>	This is used for defining text you want to be displayed as a superscript text
\<svg\>	This is used as a container of Scalable Vector Graphics (SVG)
\<table\>	This is used for representing data in tabular format or creating tables in HTML documents
\<tbody\>	This is used for representing a table's body content and is used with \<tfoot\> and \<thead\>
\<td\>	This is used for defining a table's cells where the cells contain table data
\<template\>	This is used for containing data on the client-side not to be displayed when the page loads and may use JavaScript to render later
\<textarea\>	This is used for defining multiple line output, like feedback, comment, review, etc.
\<tfoot\>	This is used to define an HTML table's footer content

\<th\>	This is used for defining an HTML table's head cell
\<thead\>	This is used to define an HTML table's header and is used with the \<tfoot\> and \<tbody\> tags
\<time\>	This is used for defining the time and date in HTML documents
\<title\>	This is used for defining an HTML document's name or title
\<tr\>	This is used for defining an HTML table's row cells
\<track\>	This is used for defining \<audio\> and \<video\> element text tracks
\<tt\>	This is used for defining teletype text – HTML5 does NOT support this
\<u\>	This is used for rendering enclosed text with underlining
\<ul\>	This is used for defining lists of unordered items
\<var\>	This is used for defining variable names used in programming or mathematical contexts

<video>*	This is used for embedding video content
<wbr>*	This is used for defining a position where a break line may be made in the text

HTML Attributes

HTML attributes are similar to the keywords you find in other languages. They are special and provide more details about elements – in short, they are used to modify HTML elements.

Every tag or element may have one or more attributes, which define the element's behavior. There are a few things you need to be aware of about attributes:

- The start tag should always be used to apply them

- They must always be applied with their name/value pair

- Names and values are case sensitive and lowercase is recommended

- HTML elements can have multiple attributes but there must be a space between them

Syntax

The syntax used for attributes is:

```
<element
attribute_name="value">content</element>
```

Here's an example:

```
<!DOCTYPE html>
<html>
<head>
</head>
<body>
    <h1> This is the Style attribute</h1>
    <p style="height: 50px; color: blue">It
adds the style property in the element</p>
    <p style="color: red">It changes the
content color</p>
</body>
</html>
```

Running this should output the following on your screen:

This is the Style attribute

It adds the style property in the element

It changes the content color

Let's break this down:

- **<p style='height: px; color: blue"> It adds the style property in the element</p>** - This statement uses the paragraph tags, in which the style property has been applied. Although this book is about HTML, this attribute is useful when you want CSS properties on an HTML element. What we did here was set a height element of 50px and changed it to blue.

- **<p style="color: red">It will changes the content color</p>** - Again, the paragraph tags are used to include the style element. This time, we turned it to red.

Next, we will look at some of the more common attributes:

The Title Attribute

This is used in most browsers as a text tooltip. When a user moves their cursor over text or a link, the text will be displayed. It can be used with any inks or text to show the relevant description. In the example below, we are using this with the paragraph and heading tags:

With the <h1> tag:

```
<h1 title="This is the heading tag">Example
of the title attribute</h1>
With <p> tag:
<p title="This is the paragraph tag">Move
the cursor over the heading and paragraph,
and the description is shown as a
tooltip</p>
```

The code example is:

```
<!DOCTYPE html>
<html>
  <head>
  </head>
<body>

  <h1 title="This is the heading
tag">Example of the title attribute</h1>
```

```
<p title="This is the paragraph tag">Move
the cursor over the heading and paragraph,
and the description is shown as a
tooltip</p>

</body>
</html>
```

On your screen, you will see the following:

Example of the title attribute

Move the cursor over the heading and paragraph, and the description is shown as a tooltip

The href Attribute

This is the <a> anchor tag's primary attribute and provides the link address for the link specified in the anchor. In short, href gives the hyperlink; if it is left blank, it stays on the same page.

Here's an example with and without the link address:

With the link address:

```
<a href="https://www.Wikipedia.com/html-
anchor">This is a link</a>
```

Without link address:

```
<a href="">This is a link</a>
```

The output will be:

Display of href attribute

Below is the link to the anchor tag; click the link and see the next page

This is a link

The src Attribute

This is one of the most important attributes for the <img> element, and, indeed, it is required. It provides the source for the image to be shown on the browser. The image can be contained in the same or a different directory, and the name or source of the image must be correct – if not, the image will not display.

```
<img src="pigswimming.jpg" height="1000"
width="504">
```

Note that this also includes the width and height attributes, defining the size of the image shown on the browser. The output will be:

Example of the src attribute

HTML images can be displayed with the help of the image tag, and the src attribute provides the image source.

Single or Double Quotes?

You should have noticed that double quotes have been used in the attributes we've looked at so far, but you may also have seen single quotes being used elsewhere. So which one should you use? It doesn't matter, so long as the opening and closing quotes match. Both of these statements are perfectly okay:

```
<a href="https://www.wikipedia.com">A link
to HTML.</a>
<a href='https://www.wikipedia.com'>A link
to HTML.</a>
```

If you are using HTML5, quotes do not need to be used around the attribute values:

```
<a href=https://www.wikipedia.com>A link to
HTML.</a>
```

Global Attributes

Global attributes are attributes common to every HTML attribute and are supported by standard elements and non-standard elements. However, while they can be used on every element, they won't affect all elements. These are the global attributes – those marked with an asterisk (*) are new to HTML5:

Attribute	Value	Description
accesskey	character	Used for generating the current element's keyboard shortcuts
class	classname	Used for providing the current element's class name and is used primarily with the stylesheet

Contenteditable*	true/ false	Used for determining whether an element's content is editable
contextmenu	menu_id	Used for defining the <menu> element id. This element is an element's context menu, appearing on a right-click
data-* *	somevalue	Used for storing private data specific to the element and accessible via JavaScript.
dir	rtl, lr, auto	Used to specify the content direction in the current element
draggable *	true, false, auto	Used for specifying if an element's content can be moved using the Drag and Drop API
dropzone	copy, move, link	Used for specifying what action should be taken on the dragged element when it gets dropped – should it be moved, copied, or linked?

hidden *		Used for hiding the element from view
id	id	Used for specifying the element's unique id
lang	language_code	Used for specifying the primary language used for the element's content
style	style	Used for applying inline CSS to an element
spellcheck *	true	Used for specifying whether content should be spell-checked
tabindex	number	Used for determining an element's tabbing order
title	text	Used for providing the element's title or name, or other relevant information
translate *	yes, no	Used for specifying whether an element's content should be localized where a page is localized

Windows Event Attributes

These event attributes must be applied using the <body> tag and are related to the window object:

Attribute	Description
onafterprint	The script is executed once the document has been printed
onbeforeprint	The script is executed before the document gets printed
onbeforeunload	The script is executed before the document is unloaded
onerror	The script is executed when an error arises
onhashchange	The script is executed when a change occurs in the anchor section of the web page URL
onload	The script is executed only after the web page has fully loaded
onmessage	The script is executed on the occurrence of a message event
onoffline	The script is executed on disconnection of the network connection, and the browser is working offline
ononline	The script is executed when the browser comes back online

onpagehide	The script is executed when the web page gets hidden, like if the user moves away from the web page
onpageshow	The script is executed when the web page becomes focused
onpopstate	The script is executed upon a change to the active history of the window
onresize	The script is executed when the window size changes
onstorage	The script is executed when an update occurs to the web storage
onunload	The script is executed when the window is closed, or the web page unloads

Form Event Attributes

These occur when an action is performed within a form by a user. This could be choosing an input field, submitting the form, and so on. While form elements can be used with all elements, they tend to be used with the HTML form elements. These are all the attributes:

Attribute	Description
onblur	The script is executed when the form element focus goes
onchange	The script is executed when element value changes
onfocus	The event is triggered when the element gets focused
oninput	The script is executed when user input is added to the element
oninvalid	The script is executed when predefined constraints are not satisfied by the element
onreset	The event is triggered when the user resets the form element values
onsearch	The event is triggered when the input goes into a search field
onselect	The event is triggered when the user selects text
onsubmit	The event is triggered on submission of the form

Keyboard Event Attributes

These events occur on interaction with the keyboard by the user. These are the keyboard events:

Attribute	Description
onkeydown	The event is triggered when the user presses a keyboard key
onkeypress	The event is triggered when a key pressed by a user displays a character
onkeyup	The event is triggered when the user releases the pressed key

Mouse Event Attributes

Attribute	Description
onclick	The event is triggered when the element is mouse-clicked
ondblclick	The event is triggered when the element is double-clicked with the mouse
onmousedown	The event is triggered when the mouse button gets clicked on the element

onmousemove	The event is triggered when the mouse pointer is moved over the element
onmouseout	The event is triggered when the mouse moves away from the element
onmouseover	The event is triggered when the mouse is moved on the element
onmouseup	The event is triggered on the release of the mouse button
onmousewheel	Deprecated – the onwheel attribute should be used
onwheel	The event is triggered when the mouse wheel is rolled down or up over the element

Clipboard Event Attributes

Attribute	Description
oncopy	The event is triggered when the user copies content to the system clipboard
oncut	The event is triggered when the content in an element is cut and copied onto the clipboard
onpaste	The event is triggered when content is pasted into an element by the user

Media Event Attributes

Attribute	Description
onabort	The script is executed when playback of media is aborted
oncanplay	The script is executed when the media file is ready for playing
oncanplaythrough	The script is executed when a media file can be played without stopping or buffering
oncuechange	The script is executed when the <track> element text cue is changed
ondurationchange	The script is executed when the duration of the media file is changed
onemptied	The script is executed if a file becomes unavailable due to a fatal error on the media
onended	The script is executed when the media file ends
onerror	The script is executed when an error occurs while the media data is being fetched

onloadeddata	The script is included when the media data has been loaded
onloadedmetadata	The script is executed when the media file's metadata is loaded
onloadstart	The script is executed when the media file begins loading
onpause	The script is executed when the playback is paused
onplay	The script is executed when a paused media file is ready to play again
onplaying	The script is executed when the media file begins playing
onprogress	The script is executed when the browser begins to retrieve the media data
onratechange	The script is executed when the playback speed changes
onseeked	The script is executed when the seek operation ends, and the seeking attribute is set as false
onseeking	The script is executed on activation of the seek operation, and the seeking attribute is set as true

onstalled	The script is executed when the browser suddenly ceases to retrieve data media
onsuspend	The script is executed if the media data fetch operation is stopped intentionally
ontimeupdate	The script is executed when a change is made to the playback position, such as fast-forwarding or rewinding a track
onvolumechange	The script is executed when the media volume changes – mute or unmute
onwaiting	The script is executed when playback pauses because more data needs to be loaded

HTML Elements

HTML files consist of elements which are used to create web pages, defining the content on them. HTML elements are usually made up of <tag name> (the start tag), content (attributes) and </tag name> (the close tag). Be aware that not all elements have content and end tags. These are called empty elements, void elements, or self-closing elements and include <hr>, <br>, and so on. Here's an example:

```
<p> Hello world!!! </p>
```

Here's an example:

```
<!DOCTYPE html>
<html>
<head>
    <title>WebPage</title>
</head>
<body>
    <h1>This is my first web page</h1>
     <h2> How does it look?</h2>
      <p>It looks great!</p>
</body>
</html>
```

The output will look like this:

This is my first web page

How does it look?

It looks great!

Note that all content between the body elements can be seen on the web page.

It should also be noted that some HTML elements can be nested, meaning elements can have other elements inside them.

Block-Level and Inline HTML Elements

In HTML, elements are placed into two categories for the purpose of styling and default display:

- Block-level

- Inline

Block-level

Block-level elements are what help structure the main space on the web page by breaking the page into logical blocks. They always begin with a new line, and they always cover the full page width, from left to right. As well as inline elements, they may also contain block-level elements.

These are the HTML block-level elements:

- <address>

- <article>

- <aside>

- <blockquote>

- <canvas>

- <dd>

- <div>

- <dl>

- <dt>

- <fieldset>

- <figcaption>

- <figure>

- <footer>

- <form>

- <h1>-<h6>

- <header>

- <hr>

- <li>

- <main>

- <nav>

- <noscript>

- <ol>

- <output>

- <p>

- <pre>

- <section>

- <table>

- <tfoot>

- <ul>

- <video>.

Here's an example:

```
<!DOCTYPE html>
<html>
```

```
                <head>
        </head>
<body>
    <div style="background-color:
lightblue">This is the first div</div>
    <div style="background-color:
lightgreen">This is the second div</div>
    <p style="background-color: pink">This
is a block level element</p>
</body>
</html>
```

The output is:

This is the first div

This is the second div

This is a block level element

In the example, we have used the <div> tag to define a web page's section, taking the entire page width. We also used the style attribute on the HTML content and the background color to show it is a block-level element.

Inline Elements

Inline elements are used to differentiate bits of the specified text and give it a function. They do not begin with a new line, and the width is taken as needed. Mostly, these are used with other elements.

These are the inline elements:

- `<a>`
- `<abbr>`
- `<acronym>`
- `<b>`
- `<bdo>`
- `<big>`
- `<br>`
- `<button>`
- `<cite>`
- `<code>`
- `<dfn>`
- `<em>`
- `<i>`
- `<img`
- `<input>`
- `<kbd>`
- `<label>`
- `<map>`
- `<object>`
- `<q>`
- `<samp>`

- <script>

- <select>

- <small>

- <span>

- <strong>

- <sub>

- <sup>

- <textarea>

- <time>

- <tt>

- <var>

Here's an example:

```
<!DOCTYPE html>
<html>
    <head>
    </head>
<body>
    <a href="https://www.wikimedia.com/html
">Click on the link</a>
    <span style="background-color:
lightblue">this is an inline element</span>
    <p>This takes the text width only</p>
 </body>
</html>
```

This is the output:

Click on the link this is an inline element

This takes the text width only

The table below shows the common HTML elements:

Start tag	Content	End tag	Description
\<h1\> ...... **\<h6\>**	HTML headings	\</h1\>??..\</h6\>	Used to provide page headings
\<p\>	Paragraph	\</p\>	Used to show the content in paragraph form
\<div\>	div section	\</div\>	Used to provide sections in web pages
\<br\>		_____	Void element – provides a line break
\<hr\>		_____	Void element – provides a horizontal line

Chapter 3

HTML Formatting

HTML gives us an easy way of formatting text to make it look and feel better without having to rely on CSS. There are plenty of HTML formatting tags, used for underlining, italicizing, and bolding text, to name just a few. There are 14 formatting tags, divided into two subcategories:

- **Physical tags** – used to give the text a physical look

- **Logical tags** – used to give the text a semantic or logical value

While some tags may look the same visually, semantically, they are different.

These are the HTML formatting tags:

Element	Description
\<b\>	Physical tag, used for bolding text written in between

\<strong\>	Logical tag, informs the browser the text has importance
\<i\>	Physical tag, used for italicizing the text
\<em\>	Logical tag, displays the content in italics
\<mark\>	Used for highlighting specified text
\<u\>	Used for underlining the specified text
\<tt\>	Used to show specified text in teletype – HTML5 does not support this
\<strike\>	Used to show a strikethrough on specified text – HTML5 does not support this
\<sup\>	Used for displaying content above the normal line
\<sub\>	Used for displaying content below the normal line
\<del\>	Used for displaying deleted content
\<ins\>	Used to show added content
\<big\>	Used for increasing font by one size unit

<small>	Use for decreasing font by one size unit from the base size

Let's look at how some of these work.

1. Bold Text

This uses two tags - <b> and <strong>

The <b> tag is physical and is used to show the text in bold with no logical or semantical importance. Anything written between the <b> tags will be displayed in bold – here's an example:

```
<p> <b>Write something in bold text.</b></p>
```

The output would be:

Write something in bold text.

The <strong> tag is logical. Not only is the text shown in bold, but the browser is also told of the logical importance of the text. Anything written between the opening and closing <strong> tags is shown as important text:

```
<p><strong>This is  important
content</strong>, while this is normal
content</p>
```

And the output is:

This is important content, while this is normal content

Here's a code example

```
<!DOCTYPE html>
<html>
<head>
    <title>formatting elements</title>
</head>
<body>
<h1>Explanation of the formatting
element</h1>
<p><strong>This is  important
content</strong>, while this is normal
content</p>
</body>
</html>
```

The output is:

Explanation of the formatting element

This is important content, while this is the normal content

2. **Italic Text**

This uses the <i> and <em> tags.

The <i> tag is physical, and it shows content written between it in italic but with no importance attached to it. Anything written between the <i> tags is shown in italics:

```
<p> <i>Write something in italic
text.</i></p>
```

This would be shown like this:

Write Your First Paragraph in italic text.

The <em> tag is logical, showing the content between the tags in italics with sematic importance added:

```
<p><em>This is  important content</em>,
displayed in italic font.</p>
```

The output is:

This is an important content, which displayed in italic font.

Here's the code:

```
<!DOCTYPE html>
<html>
<head>
    <title>formatting elements</title>
</head>
<body>
<h1>Explanation of the italic formatting
element</h1>
<p><em>This is  important content</em>,
displayed in italic font.</p>
</body>
</html>
```

The output is:

Explanation of the italic formatting element

This is important content, displayed in italic font.

3. **Marked Formatting**

We use the <mark>...</mark> tag to highlight or mark specific text. Here's an example:

```
<h2>  I want  a <mark> Mark</mark> on your
face</h2>
```

The output is:

I want to put a Mark on your face

4. Underlined Text

Anything written between the <u>...</u> tags will be displayed with an underline:

```
<p> <u>Write something in underlined
text.</u></p>
```

Here's the output:

Write something in underlined text.

5. Strike Text

If you want specific text shown with a strikethrough, use the <strike> tags. A strikethrough shows text with a thin line through it:

```
<p> <strike>Write something with a
strikethrough</strike>.</p>
```

And the output is:

Write Your First Paragraph with a strikethrough.

6. Monospaced Font

If you want each letter to be of the same width, you should place it between the <tt>...</tt> tags. You might want to do this if you are using different fonts, as many are called variable-width fonts, meaning some letters have different widths. For example, the letter 'i' is not as wide as the letter 'w.' By using monospaced font, you can ensure a uniform spacing between letters.

Here's an example:

```
<p>Hello <tt>Write something in monospaced
font.</tt></p>
```

The output is:

Hello Write something in monospaced font.

7. Superscript Text

When you use the ^{...} tags, any text in between them is displayed in superscript, meaning it is half a height above the other characters. Here's an example:

```
<p>Hello <sup>Write something in
superscript.</sup></p>
```

The output is:

Hello ^{Write something in superscript.}

8. Subscript Text

When you use the _{...} tags, any text in between is shown half a height below the other characters.

```
<p>Hello <sub>Write something in
subscript.</sub></p>
```

The output is:

Hello _{Write something in subscript.}

9. Deleted Text

Whatever text you place between the <del>…</del> tags is shown as deleted. Here's an example:

```
<p>Hello <del>Delete something.</del></p>
```

The output is:

Hello

10. Inserted Text

Any text input between the <ins>…</ins> tags is shown as inserted. Here's an example:

```
<p> <del>Delete your first
paragraph.</del><ins>Write another
paragraph.</ins></p>
```

And the output is:

 Write another paragraph.

11. Larger Text

If you want to increase some text bigger than the rest, that text should be placed between the <big>...</big> tags. It will increase the text one seize larger than the rest. Here's the example:

```
<p>Hello <big>Write something in a larger
font.</big></p>
```

The output would be:

Hello Write something in a larger font.

12. **Smaller Text**

If you want some text to be smaller than the rest, it should be placed between the <small>...</small> tags. The font is reduced by one size. Here's the example:

```
<p>Hello <small>Write something in a smaller
font.</small></p>
```

And the output is:

Hello Write something in a smaller font.

Chapter 4

Headings, Paragraphs, and Phrase Tags

HTML Heading

HTML headings are signified by the <h> tag and are defined as titles or subtitles in the content displayed on the web page. Each <h> tag has a predefined text size (although this can be changed), and any text between the tags is shown in the relevant size and bold.

There are six <h> tags, starting with <h1>, the most important and ending with <h6>, the least important. H1 has the largest tag, while h6 has the smallest. Therefore, we use h1 to signify the most important heading text and h6 for the least important.

HTML headings are helpful to search engines as they tell the engine how to understand a web page structure and index it. Be sure the use the <h1> tag for your content's main keyword.

Here's an example:

```
<h1>Heading  1</h1>
```

```
<h2>Heading 2</h2>
<h3>Heading 3</h3>
<h4>Heading 4</h4>
<h5>Heading 5</h5>
<h6>Heading 6</h6>
```

The output will look like this:

Heading 1

Heading 2

Heading 3

Heading 4

Heading 5

Heading 6

Make sure that you only use <h> tags for your content headings – they should never be used to enlarge or bold your text.

You can also use <h> tags in nested elements. Here's an example of different ways of using the heading tags:

```
<!DOCTYPE html>
<html>
 <head>
    <title>Heading tags</title>
 </head>
 <body>
    <h1>This is the main heading of the
page. </h1>
```

```
        <p>h1 is the most important , and is
used to display the page keyword  </p>
      <h2>This is the first sub-heading</h2>
        <p>h2 describes the first sub heading
one the page. </p>
      <h3>This is the second sub heading</h3>
        <p>h3 describes the second sub heading
on the page.</p>
        <p>We can use h1 to h6 tag to use
different sub-heading with paragraphs if
required.
                       </p>
    </body>
  </html>
```

The output would look like this:

This is the main heading of the page

h1 is the most important and is used to display the page keyword

This is the first sub heading

h2 describes the first sub heading on the page

This is the second sub heading

h3 describes the second sub heading on the page

We can use h1 to h6 tag to use   different sub-heading with paragraphs if required.

HTML Paragraph

The <p> tag is used to define paragraphs in the content on the web page. Let's look at a simple example, seeing how it all work. It is worth noting that browsers will add empty lines before paragraphs and after them. The <p> tag is used to indicate that a new paragraph should be started.

Note – if several <p> tags are used in one HTML file, the browser will add a blank line automatically between paragraphs. Here's the example:

```
<!DOCTYPE html>
<html>
<body>
<p>This is first paragraph.</p>
<p>This is second paragraph.</p>
<p>This is third paragraph.</p>
</body>
</html>
```

The output is:

This is the first paragraph

This is the second paragraph

This is the third paragraph

Paragraph Spaces

If you place extra spaces inside the <p> tag, accidentally or otherwise, the browser will remove them, along with extra lines, when the page is displayed. The browser will count the number of lines and spaces as one:

```
<p>
I am
Providing you with
an HTML tutorial
that is hope you will find beneficial.
</p>
<p>
Look, I added in a lot
of spaces                    but
I know that the browser will ignore them.
</p>
<p>
You cannot work out what the HTML looks
like</p>
<p>because resized windows give different
results.
</p>
```

Here's the output:

I am providing you with a tutorial on HTML that I hope you will find beneficial.

Look, I added in a lot of spaces but I know that the browser will ignore them.

You cannot work out what the HTML looks like because resized windows give different results.

Using <br> and <hr> with <p>

The <br> tag is used when you want a line break and you can include it in paragraph elements. Here is an example showing you how it works:

```
<!DOCTYPE html>
<html>
    <head>
    </head>
  <body>
      <h2> Use the line break with the
paragraph tag</h2>
             <p><br>Mama and papa, and baby and
Don,
        <br>Wanda and me? We all went to
granny's house
             <br>on Christmas day in
Bobby's sleigh.
        </p>
     </body>
</html>
```

Use the line break with paragraph tag

Mama and papa, and baby and Don,
Wanda and me? We all went to granny's house
on Christmas day in Bobby's sleigh

The <hr> tag applies a horizontal line between paragraphs or statements. Here is an example showing it being used with the <p> tag.

```
<!DOCTYPE html>
<html>
```

```
<head>
  </head>
<body>
  <h2> Example showing a horizontal line
with paragraphs</h2>
    <p> An HTML hr tag will draw a
horizontal line which will separate two
paragraphs .
<hr> a new paragraph is started.
    </p>
  </body>
</html>
```

The output of this is:

Example showing a horizontal line with paragraphs

An HTML hr tag will draw a horizontal line and separate two paragraphs with that line.

A new paragraph is started.

HTML Phrase Tag

HTML phrase tags are used to define a block of text's structural meaning or a specified text's semantics. These are all the phrase tags – you will recognize some of them from earlier:

- Abbreviation tag : <abbr>

- Acronym tag: <acronym> (HTML5 does not support this)

- Marked tag: <mark>

- Strong tag: <strong>

- Emphasized tag : <em>

- Definition tag: <dfn>

- Quoting tag: <blockquote>

- Short quote tag : <q>

- Code tag: <code>

- Keyboard tag: <kbd>

- Address tag: <address>

Let's look at these in more detail:

1. **Text Abbreviation**

We use this tag when we want some text abbreviated. That text should be placed between the <abbr> and</abbr> tags. Here's an example:

```
<p>An <abbr> title = "Hypertext Markup
language">HTML </abbr>language used for
creating web pages. </p>
```

The output is:

Hypertext Markup language

An HTML language used for creating web pages.

2. **Marked**

If you want specific content highlighted, it must be written in between the <mark> and </mark> tags will be shown highlighted in yellow in the browser. Here's an example:

```
<p>This tag will <mark>highlight</mark> the
text.</p>
```

The output is:

Example of mark tag

This tag will highlight the text.

3. **Strong**

If you want specific text displayed as important, it should be written between the <strong> and </strong> tags. Here's an example:

```
<p>In HTML you should use <strong>lower-
case</strong>, when you write code. </p>
```

The output is:

Example of strong tag

In HTML, you should use **lower-case** while writing a code.

4. **Emphasized**

If you want certain text emphasized, it should be placed between the <em> and </em> tags, and it will be displayed in italics. Here's an example:

```
<p>HTML is an <em>easy </em>language to
learn.</p>
```

The output is:

Example of emphasized tag

HTML is an *easy* language to learn.

5. Definition

The <dfn> tags are used to specify the content's main keyword. Here is an example of how to do it:

```
<p><dfn>HTML </dfn> is a markup language.
</p>
```

Here is the output:

Example of definition element

HTML is a markup language.

6. Quoting Text

When you want to show content that comes from a different source, use the <blockquote> tag. You can provide the source URL by using the cite attribute, and the source text representation goes in the <cite> tags. Here's an example:

```
<blockquote
cite="https://www.keepinspiring.me/famous-
quotes/"><p>?The first step toward success
is taken when you refuse to be a captive of
the environment in which you first find
yourself.?</p></blockquote>
<cite>-Mark Caine</cite>
```

The output is:

Example of the blockquote element

> "The first step toward success is taken when you refuse to be a captive of the environment in which you first find yourself." - *Mark Caine*

7. **Short Quotes**

If you prefer to use a shorter quotation, use the <q> tags. Any text inserted between these tags is displayed in double-quotes.

Here's an example:

```
<p>Nelson Mandela said: <q> The Greatest
Glory In Living Lies Not In Never Falling,
But In Rising Every Time We Fall.</q>?</p>
```

The output is:

Great Motivational quote

Nelson Mandela said: The Greatest Glory In Living Lies Not In Never Falling, But In Rising Every Time We Fall.

8. **Code Tags**

We can use the <code> tag to display a specific piece of computer code. The code is shown in monospaced font. Here's an example:

```
<p>First Java program</p>
<p><code>class Simple{ public static void
main(String args[]){
System.out.println("Hello Java"); }} </code>
```

</p>

The output is:

First Java program

class Simple{ public static void main(String args[]){ System.out.println("Hello Java"); }}

9. Keyboard Tag

The keyboard tag, <kbd<, is used to indicate that the specified content was input from a user on a keyboard. Here's an example:

```
<p>Please press <kbd>Ctrl</kbd> +
<kbd>Shift</kbd> + t<kbd></kbd> to restore
the page on firefox.</p>
```

Here's the output

Keyboard input.

Please press Ctrl + Shift + t to restore the page on chrome.

10. Address Tag

The address tag is used to define the content author's contact information. Any content between <address> and </address> is displayed in italics. Here's the example:

```
<address> You can contact us at <a
href="">example123@newdomain.com</a>
<br> You can also find us at: <br>1234 Pine
street, Philadelphia, Pennsylvania, PA
19100.  </address>
```

The output is:

Address Tag

You can contact us at example123@newdomain.com

You can also find us at:

1234 Pine Street, Philadelphia, Pennsylvania, PA 19100.

Chapter 5

Images, Tables, and Links

HTML Images

Everybody knows that a website filled only with text and no pictures is pretty boring, and people will soon switch it off. Adding images can significantly improve how your website looks and feels – here are some examples of images:

```
<!DOCTYPE html>
<html>
<body>

<h2>HTML Image</h2>
<img src="pic_girldancing.jpg" alt="girl
dancing" width="500" height="333">

</body>
</html>
```

This would show this followed by an image :

HTML Image

And another example:

```
<!DOCTYPE html>
<html>
<body>

<h2>HTML Image</h2>
<img src="img_girl.jpg" alt="flower garden"
width="500" height="600">

</body>
</html>
```

And the output is:

HTML Image

And the last example:

```
<!DOCTYPE html>
<html>
<body>
```

```
<h2>HTML Image</h2>
<img src="img_chania.jpg" alt="open road"
width="460" height="345">

</body>
</html>
```

And this looks like:

HTML Image

Syntax and Attributes

Embedding images on an HTML web page requires the use of the <img> tag. Technically speaking, an image is not inserted; it is linked to a web page where the image is held, and the <img> tag is a container for the reference to the image.

This is one of those tags that does not have a closing tag; it is empty and only contains attributes, of which it has two required ones:

- src – used to specify the image path

- alt – used to specify alternative for the image – more about that later

Here's the syntax:

```
<img src="url" alt="alternatetext">
```

The src Attribute

The src Attribute is used to specify the image URL or path. When you open a web page, the browser retrieves the image and puts it into the web page while it is loading. As such, you should ensure that the image stays in the same place relative to the web page; otherwise, your visitors will only see a broken link icon. If the browser fails to find the image, it will display the broken link and the alt text.

```
<img src="img_road.jpg" alt="Open road">
```

The alt Attribute

The alt attribute is another required one, and it provides an alternative text in the event the viewer cannot see the image. This could be because of a poor connection, an src attribute error, a screen reader is being used, and so on. The alt attribute's value is used to describe the image:

```
<!DOCTYPE html>
<html>
<body>
```

```
<h2>Alternative text</h2>

<p>The alt attribute is used to reflect the
content of the image so that users who can't
view the image can understand what it is
about:</p>

<img src="img_road.jpg" alt="Open road"
width="460" height="345">

</body>
</html>
```

If the browser cannot locate the image, the alt attribute value is shown instead:

```
<!DOCTYPE html>
<html>
<body>

<p> If the browser cannot locate the image,
the alt attribute value is shown
instead:</p>

<img src="wrongname.gif" alt="Open road">

</body>
</html>
```

The output is

If the browser cannot locate the image, the alt attribute value is shown instead:

Image Sizing - Width and Height

The style attribute is used for specifying the height and width of the image:

```
<!DOCTYPE html>
<html>
<body>

<h2>Image Size</h2>

<p>The style attribute is used here to
specify the image width and height:</p>

<img src="img_girl.jpg" alt="girl dancing"
style="width:500px;height:600px;">

</body>
</html>
```

The output is the following followed by an image :

Image Size

The style attribute is used here to specify the image width and height:

Or the width and height attributes can be used:

```
<img src="img_girl.jpg" alt="girl
dancing" width="500" height="600">
<!DOCTYPE html>
<html>
<body>
```

```
<h2>Image Size</h2>

<p>The width and height attributes can be
used to specify an image's height and
width:</p>

<img src="img_girl.jpg" alt="open road"
width="500" height="600">

</body>
</html>
```

The output is:

Image Size

The width and height attributes can be used to specify an image's height and width:

These attributes will always use pixels to define the image height and width.

Note – you should always specify this – if you don't, there is a high risk of the web page flickering while the image is being loaded.

Width and Height or Style?

The height, width, and style attributes are all perfectly valid, but the style attribute is the best one as it stops the image sizes from being changed by the style sheets – should you use them.

Here's an example:

```
<!DOCTYPE html>
<html>
<head>
<style>
/* This style will set all the image widths
to 100%: */
img {
  width: 100%;
}
</style>
</head>
<body>

<h2>Width/Height Attributes or Style?</h2>

<p>The width attribute is used on the first
image, set as 128 pixels. This is overridden
by the style written in the head section,
and the width is set as 100%.</p>

<img src="html5.gif" alt="HTML5 Icon"
width="128" height="128">
```

```
<p>The style attribute is used in the second
image, set as 128 pixels. The style in the
head section will not override this:</p>

<img src="html5.gif" alt="HTML5 Icon"
style="width:128px;height:128px;">

</body>
</html>
```

The output is:

Width/Height Attributes or Style?

The width attribute is used on the first image, set as 128 pixels. This is overridden by the style written in the head section, and the width is set as 100%.

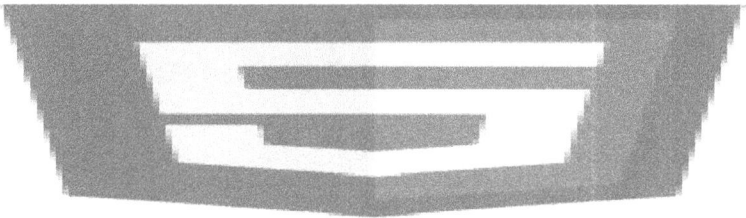

The style attribute is used in the second image, set as 128 pixels. The style in the head section will not override this:

Images in a Separate Folder

If your images are stored in a sub-folder, the folder name needs to be included in the src attribute:

```
<!DOCTYPE html>
<html>
<body>

<h2>Images in A Separate Folder</h2>
<p>Sub folders are commonly used to store
images but the folder name must be included
in the src attribute:</p>

<img src="/images/html5.gif" alt="HTML5
Icon" style="width:128px;height:128px;">

</body>
</html>
```

Output

Images in Another Folder

Sub folders are commonly used to store images, but the folder name must be included in the src attribute:

Images on a Separate Server or Website

Some pages also point to images stored on separate servers or websites. To do this, the absolute URL, which is the full URL path, must be specified in the src attribute:

```
<!DOCTYPE html>
<html>
<body>

<h2>Images on a Separate Server</h2>

<img
src="https://www.wikipedia.com/images/wikipe
dia_green.jpg" alt="Wikipedia.com"
style="width:104px;height:142px;">

</body>
</html>
```

The output is:

Images on Another Server

Animated Images

You can also include animated GIFs in HTML:

```
<!DOCTYPE html>
<html>
<body>

<h2>Animated Images</h2>

<p>HTML allows animated images:</p>

<img src="programming.gif" alt="Computer
man" style="width:48px;height:48px;">

</body>
</html>
```

The output is the following followed by an image :

Animated Images

HTML allows animated images:

Images as Links

If you want an image used as a link, the <img> tag needs to go inside the <a> tag:

```
< <!DOCTYPE html>
<html>
<body>

<h2>Image as a Link</h2>
```

```
<p>The image is a link and can be clicked
on.</p>

<a href="default.asp">
<img src="smiley.gif" alt="HTML tutorial"
style="width:42px;height:42px;">
</a>

</body>
</html>
```

The output is this followed by a smiley :

Image as a Link

The image is a link and can be clicked on.

Common Image Formats

These are the common type of image files that all browsers support:

Abbreviation	File Format	File Extension
APNG	Animated Portable Network Graphics	.apng
GIF	Graphics Interchange Format	.gif
ICO	Microsoft Icon	.ico, .cur
JPEG	Joint Photographic Expert Group image	.jpg, .jpeg, .jfif, .pjpeg, .pjp

PNG	Portable Network Graphics	.png
SVG	Scalable Vector Graphics	.svg

HTML Image Tags

- **\<img>** - used for defining images

- **\<map>** - used for defining image maps

- **\<area>** - used for defining clickable areas in image map

- **\<picture>** - used for defining containers to hold several resources for images

HTML Tables

In HTML, you have the ability to arrange your data into columns and rows:

```
<!DOCTYPE html>
<html>
<head>
<style>
table {
  font-family: arial, sans-serif;
  border-collapse: collapse;
  width: 100%;
}

td, th {
  border: 1px solid #dddddd;
```

```
    text-align: left;
    padding: 8px;
}

tr:nth-child(Ellie n) {
    background-color: #dddddd;
}
</style>
</head>
<body>

<h2>HTML Table</h2>

<table>
  <tr>
    <th>Company</th>
    <th>Contact</th>
    <th>Country</th>
  </tr>
  <tr>
    <td>Karl Werner</td>
    <td>Griselda Winters</td>
    <td>Germany</td>
  </tr>
  <tr>
    <td>Juan Carlos</td>
    <td>Margarita del Carmen</td>
    <td>Mexico</td>
  </tr>
  <tr>
    <td>Luisa Bauer</td>
    <td>Sebastian Huber</td>
    <td>Austria</td>
  </tr>
  <tr>
    <td>Semantics Co Ltd</td>
```

```
            <td>John Smith</td>
            <td>UK</td>
        </tr>
        <tr>
            <td>William Tremblay</td>
            <td>Liam Williams</td>
            <td>Canada</td>
        </tr>
        <tr>
            <td>Alessandro Berlusconi</td>
            <td>Rosa Ricci</td>
            <td>Italy</td>
        </tr>
    </table>

    </body>
    </html>
```

The output of this would be:

Company	Contact Name	Country
Karl Werner	Griselda Winters	Germany
Juan Carlos	Margarita del Carmen	Mexico
Luisa Bauer	Sebastian Huber	Austria
Semantic Co Ltd	John Smith	UK
William Tremblay	Liam Williams	Canada
Alessandro Berlusconi	Rosa Ricci	Italy

How to Define an HTML Table

Defining an HTML table is done with the <table> tag. A <tr> tag is used to define each row, while the <th> tag is used for defining the table header. Lastly, the <td> tag defines the cells/data. By default <th> tag text is in bold and centered and the <td> tag text is left aligned and regular.

Here's an example:

```
<!DOCTYPE html>
<html>
<body>

<h2>Basic HTML Table</h2>

<table style="width:100%">
  <tr>
    <th>Firstname</th>
    <th>Lastname</th>
    <th>Age</th>
  </tr>
  <tr>
    <td>Gillian</td>
    <td>Smith</td>
    <td>50</td>
  </tr>
  <tr>
    <td>Ellie </td>
    <td>Merton</td>
    <td>94</td>
  </tr>
  <tr>
    <td>John</td>
    <td>Docherty</td>
```

```
        <td>80</td>
      </tr>
    </table>

    </body>
    </html>
```

The output is:

Basic HTML Table

Firstname	Lastname	Age
Gillian	Smith	50
Ellie	Merton	94
John	Docherty	80

Note - <td> elements are containers that hold the table data and hold different HTML elements, such as other tables, images, texts, lists, etc.

Adding a Border

Many people think that you need CSS to produce borders on tables in HTML, but you don't:

Header	Header
Data	Data

The HTML code needed is:

```
<table cellspacing="3" bgcolor="#000000">
    <tr bgcolor="#ffffff">
        <th>Header</th>
        <th>Header</th>
    </tr>
    <tr bgcolor="#ffffff">
        <td>Data</td>
        <td>Data</td>
    </tr>
</table>
```

A long time ago, way back in the 90s, we used pure HTML to do what is now done by CSS, and handling visual borders were one of them. It isn't exactly about handling the borders, it's more about imitating it, and this is done by exploiting two attributes – bgcolor and cellspacing. These days, this is a perfectly good method to use, even if some do prefer to use CSS styling instead.

- We use the bgcolor attribute in the table tag to ensure the background is a specific color

- In the <tr> tag, the bgcolor attribute is used to ensure the row and column background are of a specific color but different from those of the table background.

- The cellspacing attribute in the table tag creates a space around the cells in the table. The space is given a color with the bgcolor attribute, and this will be different from the row and column background color; this creates a visual border around the cells.

Cells Spanning Multiple Columns

The colspan attribute is used for making cells span more than a single column.

Here's an example:

```
<!DOCTYPE html>
<html>
<head>
<style>
table, th, td {
  border: 1px solid black;
  border-collapse: collapse;
}
th, td {
  padding: 5px;
  text-align: left;
}
</style>
</head>
<body>

<h2>Cell spanning two columns</h2>
<p>The colspan attribute is needed to make a
cell span more than one column.</p>

<table style="width:100%">
  <tr>
```

```
  <th>Name</th>
  <th colspan="2">Telephone</th>
</tr>
<tr>
  <td>Elon Musk</td>
  <td>56776542</td>
  <td>56776541</td>
</tr>
</table>

</body>
</html>
```

The output is:

Cells Spanning Two Columns

The colspan attribute is needed to make a cell span more than one column:

Name	Telephone	
Elon Musk	56776542	56776541

Cells Spanning Multiple Rows

The rowspan attribute is used to make cells span more than one row:

```
<!DOCTYPE html>
<html>
```

```
<head>
<style>
table, th, td {
  border: 1px solid black;
  border-collapse: collapse;
}
th, td {
  padding: 5px;
  text-align: left;
}
</style>
</head>
<body>

<h2>Cell spanning two rows</h2>
<p>The rowspan attribute is needed to make a
cell span more than one row.</p>

<table style="width:100%">
  <tr>
    <th>Name:</th>
    <td>Elon Musk</td>
  </tr>
  <tr>
    <th rowspan="2">Telephone:</th>
    <td>56776542</td>
  </tr>
  <tr>
    <td>56776541</td>
  </tr>
</table>

</body>
</html>
```

The output is:

Cell spanning two rows

The rowspan attribute is needed to make a cell span more than one row:

Name:	Elon Musk
Telephone:	56776542
	56776541

Adding Captions to Tables

The <caption> tag is used to add captions to tables:

```
<!DOCTYPE html>
<html>
<head>
<style>
table, th, td {
  border: 1px solid black;
  border-collapse: collapse;
}
th, td {
  padding: 5px;
  text-align: left;
}
</style>
</head>
```

```
<body>

<h2>Table Caption</h2>
<p>The caption tag is used to add captions
to tables.</p>

<table style="width:100%">
  <caption>Monthly savings</caption>
  <tr>
    <th>Month</th>
    <th>Savings</th>
  </tr>
  <tr>
    <td>March</td>
    <td>$100</td>
  </tr>
  <tr>
    <td>April</td>
    <td>$50</td>
  </tr>
</table>

</body>
</html>
```

The output is:

Table Caption

The caption tag is used to add captions to tables.

Monthly savings

Month	Savings
March	$100
April	$50

Note that the <caption> tag is inserted straight after the <table> tag.

Special Styles for Specific Tables

If you want a specific table to have a special style, it must be defined with the <id> attribute:

```
<table id="t01">
  <tr>
    <th>Firstname</th>
    <th>Lastname</th>
    <th>Age</th>
  </tr>
  <tr>
    <td>Ellie </td>
    <td>Merton</td>
    <td>94</td>
  </tr>
</table>
```

Now a special style can be defined for the table:

```
<!DOCTYPE html>
<html>
```

```
<head>
<style>
table, th, td {
  border: 1px solid black;
  border-collapse: collapse;
}
th, td {
  padding: 15px;
  text-align: left;
}
#t01 {
  width: 100%;
  background-color: #f1f1c1;
}
</style>
</head>
<body>

<h2>Styling Tables</h2>

<table style="width:100%">
  <tr>
    <th>Firstname</th>
    <th>Lastname</th>
    <th>Age</th>
  </tr>
  <tr>
    <td>Gillian</td>
    <td>Smith</td>
    <td>50</td>
  </tr>
  <tr>
    <td>Ellie </td>
    <td>Merton</td>
    <td>94</td>
  </tr>
```

```html
      <tr>
        <td>John</td>
        <td>Docherty</td>
        <td>80</td>
      </tr>
    </table>
    <br>

    <table id="t01">
      <tr>
        <th>Firstname</th>
        <th>Lastname</th>
        <th>Age</th>
      </tr>
      <tr>
        <td>Gillian</td>
        <td>Smith</td>
        <td>50</td>
      </tr>
      <tr>
        <td>Ellie </td>
        <td>Merton</td>
        <td>94</td>
      </tr>
      <tr>
        <td>John</td>
        <td>Docherty</td>
        <td>80</td>
      </tr>
    </table>

  </body>
</html>
```

The output is:

Styling Tables

Firstname	Lastname	Age
Gillian	Smith	50
Ellie	Merton	94
John	Docherty	80

Firstname	Lastname	Age
Gillian	Smith	50
Ellie	Merton	94
John	Docherty	80

And you can add even more styles:

```
#t01 tr:nth-child(Ellie n) {
  background-color: #eee;
}
#t01 tr:nth-child(odd) {
  background-color: #fff;
}
#t01 th {
  color: white;
  background-color: black;
}
```

Adding these into the code will produce the output:

Styling Tables

Firstname	Lastname	Age
Gillian	Smith	50
Ellie	Merton	94
John	Docherty	80

Firstname	Lastname	Age
Gillian	Smith	50
Ellie	Merton	94
John	Docherty	80

HTML Table Tags

These are the HTML table tags:

Tag	Description
<table>	Used for defining tables
<th>	Used for defining a table's header cells
<tr>	Used for defining rows in tables
<td>	Used for defining cells in tables
<caption>	Used for defining table captions

<colgroup>	Used for specifying groups of columns for formatting in a table
<col>	Used for specifying properties for each column inside the <colgroup> tag
<thead>	Used for grouping the table's header content
<tbody>	Used for grouping the table's body content
<tfoot>	Used for grouping the table's footer content

HTML Links

An HTML link is a hyperlink and, when you click on one, it takes you straight to another document. You may notice that when you hover your mouse over a hyperlink, the mouse cursor change. Note that links can be text, images, or some other element in HTML.

Syntax

The <a> tag is used for defining hyperlinks:

```
<a href="url">link text</a>
```

The href attribute is the most important of the <a> tag attributes because it is used to indicate the link destination. The link text is what viewers see and, when they click on it, they are redirected to a different UTL.

Here's how to create a link to Wikipedia.com:

```
<!DOCTYPE html>
<html>
<body>

<h1>HTML Links</h1>

<p><a
href="https://www.wikipedia.com/">Visit
Wikipedia.com!</a></p>

</body>
</html>
```

The output is:

HTML Links

Visit Wikipedia.com!

By default, in all browsers, links will appear like this:

- **Underlined and Blue** – a link that hasn't been visited

- **Underlined and Purple** – a link that has been visited

- **Underlined and Red** – a link that is active

The Target Attribute

By default, the hyperlinked page is shown in the current browser window, but another target must be specified if you want to change it. The target attribute is used to specify where the link will open, and it can have any of these values:

- **_self_** - this is the default, and it opens the link in the window or tab it was clicked in.

- **_blank_** - this will open the link in a different tab or window

- **_parent_** - this will open the link in the parent frame

- **_top_** - this will open the link in the window's full body

Here's an example:

target="_blank" is used to open the link in a different tab or window:

```
<!DOCTYPE html>
<html>
<body>

<h2>The target Attribute</h2>

<a href="https://www.wikipedia.com/"
target="_blank">Visit Wikipedia!</a>

<p>If target="_blank", the link opens in a
new tab or window.</p>
```

```
</body>
</html>
```

The output is:

The target Attribute

Visit Wikipedia!

If target="_blank", the link will open in a new browser window or tab.

Absolute URLs vs. Relative URLs

Both of the above examples use the absolute URL in the href attribute, which is the full web address. If you want to use a local link, which is a link to another page on the same website, you will use a relative URL, which doesn't include the https://www bit of the address.

```
< <!DOCTYPE html>
<html>
<body>

<h2>Absolute URLs</h2>
<p><a
href="https://www.Wikipedia.com/">W3C</a></p
>
<p><a
href="https://www.google.com/">Google</a></p
>

<h2>Relative URLs</h2>
<p><a href="html_images.asp">HTML
Images</a></p>
```

```
</body>
</html>
```

The output is

Absolute URLs

Wikipedia

Google

Relative URLs

HTML Images

More examples:

Link to a webpage using a full URL

```
<!DOCTYPE html>
<html>
<body>

<h2>External Paths</h2>

<p>We are linking to a web page using a full
URL:</p>
<p><a
href="https://www.wikipedia.com/html/default
.asp">wikipedia</a></p>

</body>
</html>
```

The output is:

External Paths

We are linking to a web page using a full URL:

Wikipedia

This example will link to page in the current website's html folder:

```
<!DOCTYPE html>
<html>
<body>

<h2>External Paths</h2>

<p>We are linking to a page on the current
website's html folder:</p>

<p><a href="/html/default.asp">HTML
tutorial</a></p>

</body>
</html>
```

The output is:

External Paths

We are linking to a page on the current website's html folder

Wikipedia

And this one links to page in a folder shared by the current page:

```
<!DOCTYPE html>
<html>
<body>

<h2>External Paths</h2>

<p>We are linking to a page in a folder
shared by the current page:</p>

<p><a href="default.asp">HTML
tutorial</a></p>

</body>
</html>
```

The output is:

External Paths

We are linking to a page in a folder shared by the current page

Wikipedia

Using Images as Links

If you wanted an image used a link, the <img> tag would go inside the <a> tag. Here's an example:

```
<!DOCTYPE html>
<html>
<body>

<h2>Image as a Link</h2>

<p>The image below is a link. Try to click
on it.</p>
```

```
<a href="default.asp"><img src="smiley.gif"
alt="HTML tutorial"
style="width:42px;height:42px;"></a>

</body>
</html>
```

The output is this followed by a smiley :

Image as a Link

The image below is a link. Try to click on it.

Linking to an Email Address

You can also create a link for your visitors to click, which will open their email program so they can send an email – this is done using mailto: in the href attribute.

Here's an example:

```
<!DOCTYPE html>
<html>
<body>

<h2>Link to Email Address</h2>

<p>Use mailto: in the href attribute to
create a link opening the user's email
program (so they can send an email):</p>

<p><a href="mailto:someone@example.com">Send
email</a></p>
```

```
</body>
</html>
```

The output is:

Link to an Email Address

Use mailto: in the href attribute to create a link opening the user's email program (so they can send an email):

Send email

Link Titles

You can use the title attribute if you want extra details specified about an element. Mostly, the information will be shown as a tooltip when the user hovers their mouse over that element:

```
<!DOCTYPE html>
<html lang="en-US">
<body>

<h2>Link Titles</h2>
<p>Use the title attribute to show extra
information about a specific element. This
will be shown as a tooltip when the mouse
cursor is hovered over the element.</p>
<a href="https://www.wikipedia.com/html/"
title="Go to Wikipedia HTML section">Visit
Wikipedia</a>

</body>
</html>
```

The output is:

Link Titles

Use the title attribute to show extra information about a specific element. This will be shown as a tooltip when the mouse cursor hovers over the element:

Visit Wikipedia

HTML Link Tags

There is one link tag that you need to be aware of:

- <a> - used for defining a hyperlink

Chapter 6

HTML Lists

In HTML, lists are used as a way of specifying lists containing. Lists can have multiple elements, and there are three types of list in HTML:

1. Ordered or numbered lists – ol

2. Unordered or bulleted lists – ul

3. Description or definition lists – dl

It is also worth noting that lists can be created within lists, known as nested lists. Let's look at these list types in more detail.

Ordered or Numbered Lists (ol)

In an ordered or numbered list, all the items in the list are marked, by default, with numbers. The <ol> tag starts the numbered list and the <li> tag is used to start the list of items:

```
<!DOCTYPE>
<html>
<body>
<ol>
 <li>Libra</li>
```

```
<li>Poker</li>
<li>Capricorn</li>
<li>Oracle</li>
</ol>
</body>
</html>
```

The output is:

1. Libra

2. Poker

3. Capricorn

4. Oracle

Ordered lists can be used for representing lists in alphabetical, numerical, or any other format where an order is required. Numbered lists fall under five types:

1. Numeric, i.e., 1, 2, 3, etc.

2. Capitan Roman Numerals, i.e., I, II, III, etc.

3. Small Roman Numerals, i.e., i, ii, iii, etc.

4. Capital Alphabetical, i.e., A, B, C, etc.

5. Small Alphabetical, i.e., a, b, c, etc.

The <ol> tag can take five types of attribute to represent the five types of list:

Type	Description
Type "1"	Default – all items in the list are ordered using numbers
Type "I"	Capitalized Roman numerals are used to order the list
Type "i"	Lowercase Roman numerals are used to order the list
Type "A"	Capitalized letters are used to order the list
Type "a"	Lowercase letters are used to order the list

Here's an example of an ordered list showing a numbered list of four topics. Note that type=]"1" is not defined because it is the default and doesn't need to be defined:

```
<!DOCTYPE html>
<html>
<body>
<ol>
 <li>HTML</li>
 <li>Java</li>
 <li>JavaScript</li>
 <li>SQL</li>
</ol>
</body>
</html>
```

The output is:

1. HTML

2. Java

3. JavaScript

4. SQL

ol type="I"

And the same list displayed with the capitalized Roman numerals:

```
<!DOCTYPE html>
<html>
<body>
<ol type="I">
  <li>HTML</li>
  <li>Java</li>
  <li>JavaScript</li>
  <li>SQL</li>
</ol>
</body>
</html>
```

The output is:

I.   HTML

II. Java

III. JavaScript

IV. SQL

ol type="i"

And in lowercase Roman numerals:

```
<!DOCTYPE html>
<html>
<body>
<ol type="i">
 <li>HTML</li>
 <li>Java</li>
 <li>JavaScript</li>
 <li>SQL</li>
</ol>
</body>
</html>
```

The output is:

   i.   HTML

  ii.   Java

 iii.   JavaScript

 iv.   SQL

ol type="A"

In capitalized letters:

```
<!DOCTYPE html>
<html>
<body>
<ol type="A">
 <li>HTML</li>
 <li>Java</li>
```

```
 <li>JavaScript</li>
 <li>SQL</li>
</ol>
</body>
</html>
```

The output is:

A. HTML

B. Java

C. JavaScript

D. SQL

ol type="a"

And lastly, in lowercase letters:

```
<!DOCTYPE html>
<html>
<body>
<ol type="a">
 <li>HTML</li>
 <li>Java</li>
 <li>JavaScript</li>
 <li>SQL</li>
</ol>
</body>
</html>
```

The output is:

a. HTML

b. Java

c. JavaScript

d. SQL

Start Attribute

This attribute is used with the <ol> tag and specifies where the items in the list should begin:

> **<ol type="1" start="5">** : Shows numeric values beginning with "5".

> **<ol type="A" start="5">** : Shows capital alphabets beginning with "E".

> **<ol type="a" start="5">** : Shows lower case alphabets beginning with "e".

> **<ol type="I" start="5">** : Shows Roman upper case value beginning with "V".

> **<ol type="i" start="5">** : Shows Roman lower case value beginning with "v".

```
<!DOCTYPE html>
<html>
<body>
<ol type="i" start="5">
 <li>HTML</li>
 <li>Java</li>
 <li>JavaScript</li>
 <li>SQL</li>
```

```
</ol>
</body>
</html>
```

The output is:

   v.   HTML

  vi.   Java

 vii.   JavaScript

viii.   SQL

Reversed Attribute

The reversed attribute is Boolean and, when it is used with the <ol> tag, it reverses the list in descending order:

```
<!DOCTYPE html>
<html>
 <head>
  </head>
 <body>
 <ol reversed>
   <li>HTML</li>
    <li>Java</li>
    <li>JavaScript</li>
    <li>SQL</li>
  </ol>
 </body>
</html>
```

The output is:

4.   SQL

3.   JavaScript

2.   Java

1.   HTML

Unordered or Bulleted Lists (ul)

In an unordered or bulleted list, bullet points are used to mark the items in the list. The <ul> tag is used to start the unordered list and the <li> tag is used to start the list of items:

```
<!DOCTYPE>
<html>
<body>
<ul>
 <li>Libra</li>
 <li>Poker</li>
 <li>Capricorn</li>
 <li>Oracle</li>
</ul>
</body>
</html>
```

The output is:

o   Libra

o   Poker

o   Capricorn

o   Oracle

The unordered or bulleted list can be used when we don't need the list items shown in any specific order. There are four types of a bulleted list:

- disc

- circle

- square

- none

The <ul> tag has four attribute types to represent the different list formats:

Type	Description
"disc"	Default – a bullet point is used to mark the items in the list
"circle"	A circle is used to mark the items on the list
"square"	A square is used to mark the items on the list
"none"	There is nothing marking the list items – they are unmarked

Here's an example of the default bullet style:

```
<!DOCTYPE html>
<html>
<body>
<ul>
 <li>HTML</li>
 <li>Java</li>
 <li>JavaScript</li>
 <li>SQL</li>
</ul>
</body>
</html>
```

The output is:

- HTML

- Java

- JavaScript

- SQL

ul type="circle"

And the circle format:

```
<!DOCTYPE html>
<html>
<body>
<ul type="circle">
 <li>HTML</li>
 <li>Java</li>
 <li>JavaScript</li>
 <li>SQL</li>
```

```
  </ul>
 </body>
</html>
```

The output is:

- o HTML

- o Java

- o JavaScript

- o SQL

ul type="square"

And the square format:

```
<!DOCTYPE html>
<html>
<body>
<ul type="square">
 <li>HTML</li>
 <li>Java</li>
 <li>JavaScript</li>
 <li>SQL</li>
</ul>
</body>
</html>
```

The output is:

- ☐ HTML

- ☐ Java

☐ JavaScript

☐ SQL

ul type="none"

And the "none" format

```
<!DOCTYPE html>
<html>
<body>
<ul type="none">
 <li>HTML</li>
 <li>Java</li>
 <li>JavaScript</li>
 <li>SQL</li>
</ul>
</body>
</html>
```

The output is:

HTML

Java

JavaScript

SQL

Description or Definition Lists

The description or definition list style is supported in HTML and XHTML and the entries are listed similar to an encyclopedia or dictionary. This type of list is best used when you want a list of terms, a glossary or some other list of names and values and it contains three tags:

1. **<dl> tag** – used to define the beginning of the list.

2. **<dt> tag** – used to define terms.

3. **<dd> tag** – used to define the "definition" term (a description).

```
<!DOCTYPE>
<html>
<body>
<dl>
   <dt>Libra</dt>
   <dd>-A horoscope sign.</dd>
   <dt>Poker</dt>
   <dd>-One of my favorite weekend games</dd>
  <dt>Capricorn</dt>
  <dd>-Another horoscope sign.</dd>
   <dt>Oracle</dt>
   <dd>-A multinational technology
corporation.</dd>
</dl>
</body>
</html>
```

The output is:

Libra

-A horoscope sign.

Poker

-One of my favorite weekend games

Capricorn

-Another horoscope sign.

Oracle

-A multinational technology corporation.

Here's another example:

```
<!DOCTYPE html>
<html>
<body>
<dl>
   <dt>HTML</dt>
   <dd>is a markup language</dd>
   <dt>Java</dt>
   <dd>is a programming platform and
language</dd>
 <dt>JavaScript</dt>
 <dd>is a scripting language</dd>
   <dt>SQL</dt>
   <dd>is a query language</dd>
</dl>
</body>
</html>
```

The output is:

HTML

is a markup language

Java

is a programming platform and language

JavaScript

is a scripting language

SQL

is a query language

Nested List

Lists within lists are called nested lists. You can have any type of lists inside another list, such as unordered lists inside ordered lists.

```html
<!DOCTYPE html>
<html>
<head>
    <title>Nested list</title>
</head>
<body>
    <p>List of African countries and capital
cities</p>
<ol>
    <li>Somalia
        <ul>
            <li>Mogadishu</li>
```

```
            </ul>
        </li>
        <li>Ethiopia
            <ul>
                <li>Adis Ababa</li>
            </ul>
        </li>
        <li>Gambia
            <ul>
                <li>Banjul</li>
            </ul>
        </li>
        <li>Sierra Leone
            <ul>
                <li>Freetown</li>
            </ul>
        </li>
        <li>Angola
            <ul>
                <li>Luanda</li>
            </ul>
        </li>
        <li>Morocco
            <ul>
                <li>Rabat</li></ul>
        </li>
    </ol>
    </body>
    </html>
```

The output is:

List of African countries and capital cities

1. Somalia

- o   Mogadishu

2. Ethiopia

   - o   Adis Ababa

3. Gujarat

   - o   Banjul

4. Sierra Leone

   - o   Freetown

5. Maharashtra

   - o   Luanda

6. Morocco

   - o   Rabat

Chapter 7

HTML Forms

HTML forms are sections of documents containing controls. These could be menus, checkboxes, password fields, radio buttons, text fields, submit buttons, and so on. These forms help the user input required data, including name, password, email address, phone number, etc. They are a requirement if you want certain data collected from your website visitors. For example, let's say a user wants to make a purchase from your website. They would need to provide you with a shipping address, name, payment details, and so on to ensure that the order can be fulfilled correctly.

HTML Form Syntax

The syntax for including forms is:

```
<form action="server url" method="get|post">
    //input controls e.g. textfield, textarea,
radiobutton, button
</form>
```

HTML Form Tags

These are the tags use with HTML forms:

Tag	Description
<form>	Used to define HTML forms for the user to enter inputs
<input>	Used to define input controls
<textarea>	Used to define a control from multi-line input
<label>	Used to define labels for input elements
<fieldset>	Used to group related elements in forms
<legend>	Used to define captions for <fieldset> elements
<select>	Used to define drop-down lists
<optgroup>	Used to define groups of options that are related in drop-down lists
<option>	Used to define drop-down list options
<button>	Used to define clickable buttons

HTML 5 Form Attributes

And these are the attributes you can use with the form tags:

Tag	Description
<datalist>	Used to specify pre-defined input control options
<keygen>	Used to define a field to generate key-pairs in forms
<output>	Used to define calculation results

<form> Element

As said earlier, the <form> element provides users with a way of inputting requested information and provides different controls to allow this, including password fields, text areas, text fields, and so on. It is worth noting that the <form> element on its own will not create the form; it is a container used to hold the elements that make up the form.

<input> Element

This is one of the most fundamental form elements and is used for creating the form fields where the user inputs their information. Different input fields can be applied, depending on the information required. Here is an example showing a simple text input:

```
<body>
  <form>
```

```
    Input your name  <br>
    <input type="text" name="username">
  </form>
</body>
```

The output is:

Input your name

```
┌─────────────────────────────────────┐
│                                       │
│                                       │
└─────────────────────────────────────┘
```

TextField Control

The input tag's type="text" attribute is used to create a textfield control that is also called the single line control. While it is optional to add the name attribute, server-side components, such as PHO, ASP, JSP, and so on, require it.

```
<form>
    First Name: <input type="text"
name="firstname"/> <br/>
    Last Name:  <input type="text"
name="lastname"/> <br/>
  </form>
```

This is the output:

First Name: [   ]

Last Name: [   ]

If the name attribute is left out, the text field input doesn't get sent to the server.

<textarea> Tag

This tag is used when you want multiple-line text in your form. The <textarea> size is specified using the "cols" or "rows" attributes. Here's an example:

```
<!DOCTYPE html>
<html>
<head>
    <title>Form in HTML</title>
</head>
<body>
  <form>
        Input your address:<br>
        <textarea rows="2"
cols="20"></textarea>
  </form>
</body>
</html>
```

The output is:

Input your address:

```



```

Label Tag

Best practice says that you should have labels in your form as it ensures the code is more user, browser and parser-friendly. When the label tag is clicked on, the text control comes under focus. Doing this requires that the label tag has an attribute that matches the input tag's id attribute.

```
<form>
    <label for="firstname">First Name:
</label> <br/>
                <input type="text"
id="firstname" name="firstname"/> <br/>
    <label for="lastname">Last Name: </label>
                <input type="text"
id="lastname" name="lastname"/> <br/>
 </form>
```

The output is:

First Name:

```
┌─────────────────────────────────────────┐
│                                         │
│                                         │
└─────────────────────────────────────────┘
```

Last Name:

```
┌─────────────────────────────────────────┐
│                                         │
│                                         │
└─────────────────────────────────────────┘
```

Password Field Control

With the password field control, the user cannot see the password:

```
<form>
    <label for="password">Password: </label>
                <input type="password"
id="password" name="password"/> <br/>
</form>
```

The output is:

Password:
```
┌─────────────────────────────────┐
│                                 │
└─────────────────────────────────┘
```

Email Field Control

This is new to HTML5 and is used for validating that a user has entered a valid email address. This field must contain @ and . (period).

```
<form>
    <label for="email">Email: </label>
                <input type="email" id="email"
name="email"/> <br/>
</form>
```

You should see this in your browser:

Email: [   ]

If an incorrect email address is input, an error message like this will show on your screen:

Email: [Example.com   ]

Please include @ in the email address

Radio Button Control

Radio buttons are useful for giving users multiple options to choose from, such as quizzes, choosing gender, etc. If you choose to name all the radio buttons as one name, only one can be selected at any one time:

```
<form>
    <label for="gender">Gender: </label>
                <input type="radio"
id="gender" name="gender" value="male"/>Male
```

```
                    <input type="radio"
id="gender" name="gender"
value="female"/>Female <br/>
</form>
```

The output of this would look like this on your browser:

Gender: Male ● Female

Checkbox Control

Checkbox control is used when your users can check more than option from multiple checkboxes:

```
<form>
Hobby:<br>
                <input type="checkbox"
id="baseball" name="baseball"
value="baseball"/>
                <label
for="baseball">Baseball</label> <br>
                <input type="checkbox"
id="basketball" name="basketball"
value="basketball"/>
                <label
for="basketball">Basketball</label> <br>
                <input type="checkbox"
id="lacrosse" name="lacrosse"
value="lacrosse"/>
```

```
            <label
for="lacrosse">Lacrosse</label>
</form>
```

These are much like the radio buttons but can be used for choosing more than one option at a time – radio buttons can only be used for one option at a time.

The output from the above code would be:

Hobby:

☑ Baseball

☑ Basketball

☐ Lacrosse

Submit Button Control

In HTML, <input type="submit"> is used when a submit button is needed on a web page, such as when registering an account or signing up to a mailing list, for example. When the submit button is clicked, the user's input is sent to the server. The syntax is:

```
<input type="submit" value="submit">
```

To break this down:

- **type="submit"** – specifies the use of the submit button

- **value attribute** – whatever you choose to write on the button

- **name attribute** – may be omitted

Here's an example:

```
<form>
    <label for="name">Input name</label><br>
    <input type="text" id="name"
name="name"><br>
    <label for="pass">Input
Password</label><br>
    <input type="Password" id="pass"
name="pass"><br>
    <input type="submit" value="submit">
</form>
```

The output of this is:

Input name

```
┌─────────────────────────────────────────┐
│                                           │
│                                           │
└─────────────────────────────────────────┘
```

Input Password

```
┌─────────────────────────────────────────┐
│                                           │
│                                           │
└─────────────────────────────────────────┘
┌──────────────────┐
│  Submit          │
└──────────────────┘
```

<fieldset> Element

The <fieldset> element is used when you want related information grouped together in a form. The <legend> element is used with this to provide the grouped elements with a caption.

Here's an example:

```
<form>
    <fieldset>
      <legend>User Information:</legend>
      <label for="name">Input name</label><br>
<input type="text" id="name"
name="name"><br>
<label for="pass">Input Password</label><br>
<input type="Password" id="pass"
name="pass"><br>
<input type="submit" value="submit">
</fieldset>
```

lt;/form>

The output from this is:

User Information:

Input name:

```
┌─────────────────────────────────┐
│                                 │
│                                 │
│                                 │
└─────────────────────────────────┘
```

Input Password:

```
┌─────────────────────────────────┐
│                                 │
│                                 │
├───────────────────┐             │
│  Submit           │             │
└───────────────────┴─────────────┘
```

HTML Form Example

Here is a full example of a simple registration form:

```
<!DOCTYPE html>
```

```html
<html>
<head>
 <title>Form in HTML</title>
</head>
<body>
    <h2>Registration form</h2>
    <form>
    <fieldset>
        <legend>User personal
information</legend>
        <label>Input your full
name</label><br>
        <input type="text" name="name"><br>
         <label>Input your email</label><br>
        <input type="email"
name="email"><br>
        <label>Input your
password</label><br>
        <input type="password"
name="pass"><br>
        <label>confirm your
password</label><br>
        <input type="password"
name="pass"><br>
        <br><label>Input your
gender</label><br>
        <input type="radio" id="gender"
name="gender" value="male"/>Male  <br>
        <input type="radio" id="gender"
name="gender" value="female"/>Female <br/>
        <input type="radio" id="gender"
name="gender" value="others"/>others <br/>
         <br>Input your Address:<br>
        <textarea></textarea><br>
        <input type="submit" value="sign-
up">
```

```
            </fieldset>
          </form>
        </body>
      </html>
```

On your screen, you would see something like this:

Registration form

┌─ User personal information ─────────────────────────────────────
  Enter your full name

  Enter your email

  Enter your password

  confirm your password

  Enter your gender
    ◦ Male
    ◦ Female
    ◦ others

  Enter your Address:

  sign-up

HTML Form Input Types

One of the most important elements in an HTML form is <input type="">. An input element can have various types of "type" attributes, which are used to define the information field. For example, <input type="text" name="name"> will provide a text box.

These are the different <input> element types in HTML:

type=""	Description
text	Used to define an input field for a single line of text

password	Used to define an input field for a single line password
submit	Used to define a submit button that sends the form to the server
reset	Used to define a reset button, allowing form values to be reset
radio	Used to define a radio button allowing one option to be selected
checkbox	Used to define a checkbox, allowing multiple options to be selected
button	Used to define a push-button, programmable to perform a specified task on a given event
file	Used to define a way of selecting files from storage on the device
image	Used to define submit buttons with a graphical representation

In HTML5, a further 10 new types have been added to the <input> element:

type=""	Description
color	Used to define input fields with specified colors
date	Used to define input fields to select the date
datetime-local	Used to define input field that allows the date to be entered without a time zone
email	Used to define input fields for email addresses
month	Used to define month and year controls with no time zone
number	Used to define input fields for entering numbers
url	Used to define input fields for URLs
Week	Used to define input fields for the date using week and year, with no time zone
Search	Use to define a one-line text field for search strings
Tel	Used to define input fields for telephone numbers

Here are some examples of the <input> element:

```
<input type="text">:
<input> element of type "text" are used for
defining one-line input text fields.
<form>
    <label>Input first name</label><br>
    <input type="text" name="firstname"><br>
    <label>Input last name</label><br>
    <input type="text" name="lastname"><br>
    <p><strong>Note:</strong>The default
maximum cahracter lenght is 20.</p>
</form>
```

The output of this would be:

Input "text" type:

The **"text"**field defines a one-line input text field.

Top of Form

```
Input first name
```

```
Input last name
```

Note: The default maximum character length is 20.

<input type="password">:

The "password <input> element type lets users securely input their passwords, with text being converted to "*" or "." so other people cannot read it. Here's an example:

```
<form>
    <label>Input User name</label><br>
    <input type="text" name="firstname"><br>
    <label>Input Password</label><br>
    <input type="Password"
name="password"><br>
    <br><input type="submit" value="submit">
</form>
```

The output is:

Input "password" type:

The **"password"**field defines a one-line input password field to input the password securely.

Top of Form

Input User name

Input Password

<input type="submit">:

This type of element is used for defining submit buttons that, when the click event happens, submit forms to the server. Here's an example:

```
<form action="https://www.wikipedia.com/ ">
    <label>Input User name</label><br>
```

```
        <input type="text" name="firstname"><br>
        <label>Input Password</label><br>
        <input type="Password"
    name="password"><br>
        <br><input type="submit" value="submit">
    </form>
```

The output is:

Input "submit" type:

```
    Top of Form
    Input User name
```

```
    Input Password
```

- Once the Submit button is clicked, the form is submitted to the server, and the page is redirected to an **action** value.

-

<input type="reset">:

This type also gets defined as a button but, this time when it is clicked by the user, all values input into the form are rest to their default values. Here's an example:

<form>

```html
<label>User id: </label>
    <input type="text" name="user-id"
value="user">
                <label>Password: </label>
    <input type="password" name="pass"
value="pass"><br><br>
        <input type="submit" value="login">
        <input type="reset" value="Reset">
</form>
```

Here is the output:

```
Input "reset" type:
Top of Form

User id: [_____]   Password: [_____]

[___][___]
```

When you input user id and password values and click the button, the input fields are reset to default.

<input type="radio">:

The "radio" type of <input> is used to define radio buttons that let users choose one option from several related ones. Only one option at a time can be selected. Here's an example:

```html
<form>
    <p>Please choose your favorite color</p>
```

```
<input type="radio" name="color"
value="white"> White <br>
<input type="radio" name="color"
value="yellow"> yellow <br>
<input type="radio" name="color"
value="black">black <br>
<input type="radio" name="color"
value="red">red <br>
<input type="submit" value="submit">
</form>
```

The output is:

Input "radio" type

Top of Form

```
Please choose your favorite color
```

White

yellow

black

red

<input type="checkbox">:

The "checkbox" type of <input> shows square boxes that a user can uncheck or check to choose options form a series of given ones. These are similar to radio buttons but radio buttons only allow a user to choose one option at any one time, whereas checkbox buttons let them choose more than one. Here's an example:

```
<form>
        <label>Input your Name:</label>
        <input type="text" name="name">
        <p>Please choose your favorite
sports</p>
        <input type="checkbox" name="sport1"
value="baseball">Baseball<br>
        <input type="checkbox" name="sport2"
value="tennis">Tennis<br>
        <input type="checkbox" name="sport3"
value="basketball">Basketball<br>
        <input type="checkbox" name="sport4"
value="baseball">Baseball<br>
        <input type="checkbox" name="sport5"
value="badminton">Badminton<br><br>
        <input type="submit" value="submit">
    </form>
```

The output is:

Input "checkbox" type

Registration Form

Top of Form

Input your Name: [_____]

        Please choose your favorite sports
        [ ] Baseball
        [ ] Tennis

158

Basketball

Baseball

Badminton

<input type="button">:

This is used to define simple push buttons which can then be programmed to control an event functionality, such as what happens on a click event. While this works mostly with JavaScript, it will work on HTML, too:

```
<form>
    <input type="button" value="Click me "
onclick="alert('you are learning HTML')">
</form>
```

The output is:

Input "button" type.

Click the button to see the result:

<input type="file">:

The "file" <input> type is used when you want a user to choose one or more files from their own device storage. When the file has been selected and submitted, it can then be uploaded to the server but this requires the file API and some JavaScript code, which is outside the scope of this book.

```
<form>
    <label>Choose file to upload:</label>
    <input type="file" name="newfile">
    <input type="submit" value="submit">
</form>
```

The output is:

Input "file" type.

Choose any file type, and the chosen file will be shown beside the "choose file" option:

We can choose any type of file until we do not specify it! The selected file will appear next to the "choose file" option

Top of Form

```
Choose a file to upload:
```

<input type="image">:

This type of <input> element represents submit buttons with graphical images:

```
<!DOCTYPE html>
<html>
<body>
<h2>Input "image" type.</h2>
<p>Images can be created as submit
button</p>
   <form>
     <label>User id:</label><br>
       <input type="text" name="name"><br><br>
       <input type="image" alt="Submit"
src="login.png"  width="100px">
   </form>

  </body>
</html>
```

New HTML5 <input> Element Types

<input type="color">:

This defines input fields with colors in them and lets users specify which color they want using a visual interface in their browser. Be aware that "color" will only support hexadecimal format color values, with the default being #000000 (black):

```
<form>
    Choose your Favorite color: <br><br>
    <input type="color" name="upclick"
value="#a52a2a"> Upclick<br><br>
    <input type="color" name="downclick"
value="#f5f5dc"> Downclick
</form>
```

The output is:

Input "color" types:

Top of Form

Choose your Favorite color:

Up-click

Down-click

<input type="date">:

The "date" <input> element will generate an input field where the user can input a data in the specified format. The date can be input in two ways – via the text field or using an interface to pick a date.

```
<form>
    Choose Start and End Date: <br><br>
      <input type="date" name="Startdate">
Start date:<br><br>
      <input type="date" name="Enddate"> End
date:<br><br>
      <input type="submit">
</form>
```

The output is:

Input "date" type

Top of Form

```
Choose Start and End Date:

 Start date:

 End date:
```

\<input type="datetime-local"\>:

The "datetime-local" element allows an input field to be created so users can choose the data and local time using hours and minutes, without the need to provide time zone data.

```
<form>
    <label>
        Choose the meeting schedule: <br><br>
        Choose date & time: <input
type="datetime-local" name="meetingdate">
<br><br>
    </label>
        <input type="submit">
</form>
```

The output is:

Input "datetime-local" type

Top of Form

```
Choose the meeting schedule:

Choose date & time:
```

<input type="email">:

This element type allows an input field to be created so users can input their email addresses using pattern validation. Because there are several attributes, a user can input multiple email addresses:

```
<form>
        <label><b>Input your Email-
address</b></label>
        <input type="email" name="email"
required>
        <input type="submit">
        <p><strong>Note:</strong>Users can
input more than one email address, using a
comma or whitespace to separate them, like
this: </p>
        <label><b>Input multiple Email-
addresses</b></label>
        <input type="email" name="email"
multiple>
        <input type="submit">
</form>
```

The output is:

Input "email" type

Top of Form

Input your Email-address

Note: Users can input more than one email address, using a comma or whitespace to separate them, like this:

Input multiple Email-addresses

<input type="month">:

You can use the "month" <input> type to allow users to enter the date in MM YYYY month-year format. MM is to define the month and YYYY defines the year:

```
<form>
    <label>Input your Birth Month-year:
</label>
    <input type="month" name="newMonth">
    <input type="submit">
</form>
```

The output is:

Input "month" type:

165

Top of Form

Input your Birth Month-year: [   ]

<input type="number">:

The "number" <input> element is used for creating input fields where users can input numeric values. Users can also be restricted to entering minimum or maximum values by using the attributes min and max.

```
<form>
    <label>Input your age: </label>
    <input type="number" name="num" min="50"
max="80">
      <input type="submit">
</form>
```

The input is:

Input "number" type

Top of Form

Input your age: [   ]

- ●

166

Note that the value has been restricted to between 50 and 80 characters; anything above or below that range will produce an error.

<input type="url">:

This element is used to create input fields where users can input URLs.

```
<form>
    <label>Input your website URL: </label>
    <input type="url" name="website"
placeholder="http://example.com"><br>
    <input type="submit" value="send data">
</form>
```

The output is:

```
Input "url" type
Top of Form
Input your website URL:
```

<input type="week">:

This input type will create input fields where users can chose a week and a year from a drop-down calendar and without needing to supply the time zone.

```
<form>
    <label><b>Choose your best week of the
year:</b></label><br><br>
    <input type="week" name="bestweek">
    <input type="submit" value="Send data">
</form>
```

The output is:

Input "week" type

Top of Form

Choose your best week of the year:

\<input type="search"\>:

The "search" \<input\> element will create input fields where users can input search strings. These fields are designed to be symmetrical in functional terms to the text type but can have different styles.

```
<form>
    <label>Search here:</label>
    <input type="search" name="q">
```

```
<input type="submit" value="search">
</form>
```

The output is:

Input "search" type

Top of Form

Search here: [   ]

<input type="tel">:

Using this element allows you to create input fields where users can input telephone numbers. This type has no default validation, like the email type does, because the pattern of a telephone number is different across the world.

```
<form>
        <label><b>Input your Telephone
Number(in format of xxx-xxx-
xxxx):</b></label>
        <input type="tel" name="telephone"
pattern="[0-9]{3}-[0-9]{3}-[0-9]{4}"
requiwhite>
        <input type="submit"><br><br>
    </form>
```

The output is:

Input "tel" type

Top of Form

Input your Telephone Number(in format of xxx-xxx-xxxx):

Bottom of Form

Note that the two attributes we are using here are "pattern" and "required" – these let users input numbers in specific formats and are required for when numbers need to be input into an input field.

HTML Form Attribute

HTML contains a number of attributes that can be used with the <form> element:

action Attribute

When this attribute is used in the <form> element, it defines what needs to happen in the form when it is submitted or is used as a URI, processing the information on the form.

It may be an URI you want to use in the form processing or it could be .asp, .jsp, .pho, and so on. If the attribute value is not includes, the form is processed and stays on the same page. Here's an example:

```
<form action="action.html" method="post">
<label>User Name:</label><br>
<input type="text" name="name"><br><br>
<label>User Password</label><br>
<input type="password" name="pass"><br><br>
 <input type="submit">
```

170

```
</form>
```

The output is:

Demo of action attribute of form element

Top of Form

```
User Name:
```
[input box]

```
User Password
```
[input box]

[input box]

When the Submit button is clicked, the user is redirected to another page called "action.html".

method Attribute

This attribute is used to define the HTTP method the browser uses when the form is submitted. It has possible values of:

- **post** – this is used when we want sensitive data submitted – this will not show the data submitted in the URL.

  ```
  <form action="action.html" method="post">
  ```

- **get:** This is the default value while the form is being submitted but is not secure as the data is shown in the URL once the form has been submitted:

```
<form action="action.html" method="get">
```

When the data is submitted, the entered text is shown like this:

file:///D:/HTML/action.html?name=wikipedia&pass=123

target Attribute

This attribute is used to define where the response should be opened once the form is submitted. These are the keywords used with this attribute:

- **_self:** If this is used as an attribute value, the response will only be seen on the current page:

```
<form action="action.html" method="get"
target="_self">
```

- **_blank:** If this is used as an attribute, the response is loaded on a separate page.

```
<form action="action.html" method="get"
target="_blank">
```

autocomplete Attribute

The autocomplete attribute is new to HTML5 and is used to enable the automatic completion of input fields. There are two possible values – "on" and "off" – and these give the option of turning autocomplete on or off. The default is "on.

```
<form action="action.html" method="get"
autocomplete="on">
<form action="action.html" method="get"
autocomplete="off">
```

This can be used with the <input> element and the <form> element.

enctype Attribute

This attribute is used to define the form-content's encoding type when the form gets sent to the server. It's possible values are:

- **application/x-www-form-urlencoded:** this is the default type when the enctype attribute has been omitted from the form. Encoding of all the characters is done before the form is submitted.

```
<form action="action.html" method="post"
enctype="application/x-www-form-urlencoded"
>
```

- **multipart/form-data:** no character will be encoded and it is used when form-upload controls are present in the form.

```
<form action="action.html" method="post"
enctype="multipart/form-data">
```

- **text/plain (HTML5):** this type will only encode spaces into the + symbol; no other special characters will be encoded.

```
<form action="action.html" method="post"
enctype="text/plain" >
```

173

novalidate Attribute HTML5

This is another attribute newly added to HTMK5 and is a Boolean. If the novalidate attribute is applied in <form> no validation is performed and the form is submitted.

```
<!DOCTYPE html>
<html>
    <body>
        <h2>Fill the form</h2>
        <form action = "action.html" method =
"get" novalidate>
            Input name:<br><input type="name"
name="name"><br>
            Input age:<br><input type="number"
name="age"><br>
            Input email:<br><input type="email"
name="email"><br>
            <input type="submit"
value="Submit">
        </form>
<p><b>Try changing the details on the form
using the novalidate attribute and see what
the difference is.</b></p>
    </body>
</html>
```

The output is:

Fill the form

Top of Form

Input name:

Input age:
Input email:

Try changing the details on the form using the novalidate attribute and see what the difference is

<input> Element Attribute

name attribute

The name attribute is used to define an input element's name. The HTTP request contains the name and value attribute when the form is submitted. This attribute should not be omitted because the HTTP request has the name-value pair when the form is submitted. If name is omitted, the input field will not be processed.

```
<form action = "action.html" method = "get">
        Input name:<br><input type="name"
name="uname"><br>
        Input age:<br><input type="number"
name="age"><br>
        Input email:<br><input
type="email"><br>
        <input type="submit"
value="Submit">
    </form>
```

The output is:

Fill the form

```
Top of Form
Input name:

Input age:

Input email:
```

When Submit is clicked on, the URL will not include the email address in the HTTP request because the name attribute has not been used in this particular field.

value Attribute

This attribute is used to define an input field's initial or default value.

```
<form>
        <label>Input your Name</label><br>
        <input type="text" name="uname"
value="Input Name"><br><br>
        <label>Input your Email-
address</label><br>
        <input type="text" name="uname"
value="Input email"><br><br>
        <label>Input your
password</label><br>
```

```
        <input type="password" name="pass"
value=""><br><br>
        <input type="submit" value="login">
    </form>
```

The output is:

Fill the form

Top of Form

Input your Name

Input your Email-address

Input your password

Bottom of Form

The value attribute will always clear itself in the password input field.

required Attribute HTML5

This attribute is Boolean and is used to specify that a field must be completed before the form is submitted:

```
<form>
        <label>Input your Email-
address</label><br>
        <input type="text" name="uname"
required><br><br>
         <label>Input your
password</label><br>
        <input type="password"
name="pass"><br><br>
        <input type="submit" value="login">
    </form>
```

The output is:

Fill the form

Top of Form

```
Input your Email-address
```

```
Input your password
```

If the email field is not completed when the form is submitted, an error message will appear.

autofocus Attribute HTML5

Another Boolean attribute, this enables fields to be focused automatically after a web page loads.

```
<form>
        <label>Input your Email-
address</label><br>
        <input type="text" name="uname"
autofocus><br><br>
         <label>Input your
password</label><br>
        <input type="password"
name="pass"><br><br>
        <input type="submit" value="login">
    </form>
```

placeholder Attribute HTML5

Placeholder is used to specify text in a field that tells the user what they are expected to input. It can be used with password, text, URL, and email values and, when value is entered, the placeholder is removed.

```
<form>
        <label>Input your name</label><br>
        <input type="text" name="uname"
placeholder="Your name"><br><br>
            <label>Input your Email
address</label><br>
        <input type="email" name="email"
placeholder="example@gmail.com"><br><br>
            <label>Input your
password</label><br>
        <input type="password" name="pass"
placeholder="your password"><br><br>
```

```
<input type="submit" value="login">
</form>
```

The output is:

Registration form

Top of Form

```
Input your name
```

```
Input your Email address
```

```
Input your password
```

disabled Attribute

This attribute will disable the input field it is applied on, meaning users have no way of interacting with the field. It cannot receive any click events and, when the form is submitted, the values are not sent to the server.

```
<!DOCTYPE html>
<html>
<body>
                        <h3>Registration
form</h3>
                        <form>
```

```
                              <label>Input User
name</label><br>
              <input type="text" name="uname"
value="USER"  disabled><br><br>
                    <label>Input your Email
address</label><br>
              <input type="email" name="email"
placeholder="example@gmail.com"><br><br>
                    <label>Input your
password</label><br>
              <input type="password"
name="pass" placeholder="your
password"><br><br>
              <input type="submit"
value="login">
        </form>

</body>
</html>
```

The output is:

Registration form

Top of Form

```
Input User name
```

```
Input your Email address
```

```
Input your password
```

size Attribute

This attribute is used for controlling the input field size in typed characters:

```html
<label>Account holder name</label><br>
        <input type="text" name="uname"
size="40" required><br><br>
        <label>Account number</label><br>
        <input type="text" name="an"
size="30" required><br><br>
        <label>CVV</label><br>
        <input type="text" name="cvv"
size="1" required><br><br>
```

The output is:

Registration form with disabled attribute

Top of Form

Account holder name

Account number

CVV

182

form Attribute

This attribute lets a user specify an external field to the form but is still considered part of the main form.

User email: **
<input** type="email" name="email" form="fcontrol" required>**
**

```
<input type="submit"
form="fcontrol">
```

The output is:

Top of Form

User Name:

User password:

Bottom of Form

The email field is external to the form but is still part of the main form

User email:

Chapter 8

Classes, Frames, and iFrames

Class Attribute

The class attribute is used for specifying one or more class names for a specific element. Although this is HTML, JavaScript and CSS can also use the class name to work on HTML elements. In HTML documents, the class attribute name can be used with different elements.

Defining HTML Classes

Defining or creating HTML classes requires that you first define the class's style. That is done in the <head> section, using the <style> tag, like this:

```
<head>
    <style>
        .headings{
            color: lightgreen;
            font-family: cursive;
            background-color: black; }
    </style>
</head>
```

The class is named "headings" and we gave it a definitive style. The class name can be used with any HTML element where we want to provide the styling. All we do is use the following syntax:

```
<tag class="ghf"> content </tag>
Here's a full example:
<!DOCTYPE html>
<html>
<head>
    <style>
        .headings{
            color: lightgreen;
            font-family: cursive;
            background-color: black; }
    </style>
</head>
<body>
<h1 class="headings">This is the first
heading</h1>
<h2 class="headings">This is the Second
heading</h2>
<h3 class="headings">This is the third
heading</h3>
<h4 class="headings">This is the fourth
heading</h4>
</body>
</html>
```

The output is:

This is the first heading

This is the Second heading

This is the third heading

This is the fourth heading

Multiple Classes

You can also use more than one class name with an HTML element but each name should have a space separating it from the next. Here's an example of an element using two class names – "fruit" and "center":

```
<!DOCTYPE html>
<html>
<style>
.fruit {
    background-color: orange;
    color: white;
    padding: 10px;
}

.center {
    text-align: center;
}
</style>
<body>

<h2>Multiple Classes</h2>
<p>All three share the "fruit" class name
and Avocado also has the "center" class
name, aligning the text in the center.</p>

<h2 class="fruit center">Avocado</h2>
<h2 class="fruit">Banana</h2>
<h2 class="fruit">Pear</h2>

</body>
</html>
```

The output is:

Multiple Classes

All three share the "fruit" class name, and Avocado also has the "center" class name, aligning the text in the center

```
Avocado
Banana
Pear
```

As you can see, <h2>, which is the first element, is shared by both classes.

Same Class, Different Tag

The same name can also be used with different tags, such as <h2> and <p>, thus sharing a style. Here's an example:

```
<!DOCTYPE html>
<html>
<style>
.fruit {
  background-color: Orange;
  color: white;
  padding: 10px;
}
</style>
<body>
<h2>Same Class, Different Tag</h2>
<h2 class="fruit">Avocado</h2>
<p class="fruit">Avocado is the best
fruit.</p>
</body>
</html>
```

The output is:

Multiple Classes

All three share the "fruit" class name, and Avocado also has the "center" class name, aligning the text in the center

```
Avocado
Banana
Pear
```

HTML Frames

These days, modern websites have sticky menus for navigation, usually shown at the top or the side of the page as you scroll. However, while this is done using CSS these days, web browsers haven't always supported CSS. Two HTML elements can be used to provide the same page layouts where some content stayed static, and some could be scrolled through   frameset and frame.

However, frames do come with their own set of problems, the first being usability. With mobile devices and smaller displays much more popular these days, it is vital that websites provide several views that can change as per the viewport. You can manipulate a frame to provide a certain responsiveness level, but they are not really suited for responsive websites. Second is accessibility, with many assistive technologies, such as screen readers, struggling to understand websites with frames and communicate with them.

How to Create Frames

Frames has a pretty simple concept behind it:

- The frameset element is used in an HTML document in place of the body element

- The frame element is used for creating frames for the web page content

- The src attribute is used for identifying resources for loading in each frame

- And different files can be create with the relevant content for each frame.

Let's look into how all this works. To start with, we will create four HTML documents. Here's the first one:

```
<!DOCTYPE html>
<html>
    <body>
        <h1>Frame 1</h1>
        <p>Frame 1 contents</p>
    </body>
</html>
```

Save and call this frame_1.html. Create three more with much the same content and name them as frame_2, frame_3, and frame_4.

Vertical Columns

We want four vertical columns, and this requires the frameset element and the cols attribute. The attribute defines how many columns there are and their size – we want four, one to display each file, so we need four values, separated by commas, assigned to the cols attribute. We'll keep this simple and assign each frame the value of * - this ensures they are sized automatically to fill the space.

The markup will look like this:

```
<!DOCTYPE html>
<html>
<frameset cols="*,*,*,*">
    <frame src="../file_path/frame_1.html">
    <frame src="frame_2.html">
    <frame src="frame_3.html">
    <frame src="frame_4.html">
</frameset>
</html>
```

And it will render in the browser like this:

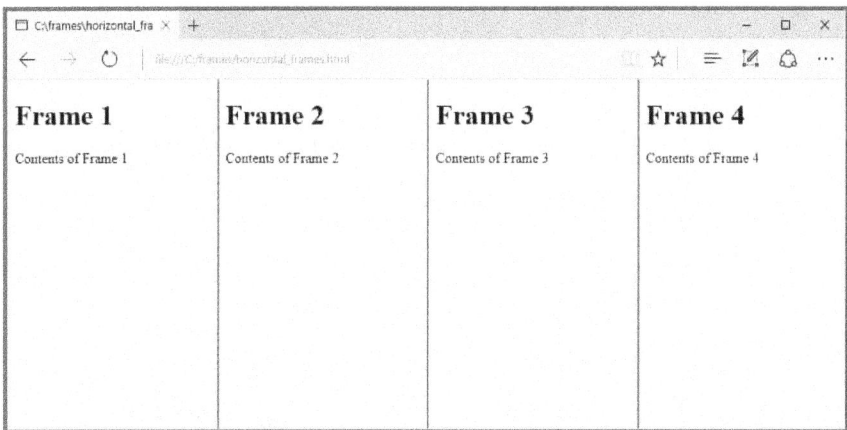

Horizontal Rows

You can use the rows attribute to create rows of frames, like this:

```
<!DOCTYPE html>
<html>
<frameset rows="*,*,*,*">
    <frame src="frame_1.html">
    <frame src="frame_2.html">
    <frame src="frame_3.html">
```

```
      <frame src="frame_4.html">
</frameset>
</html>
```

That change will load the frames in rows, like this:

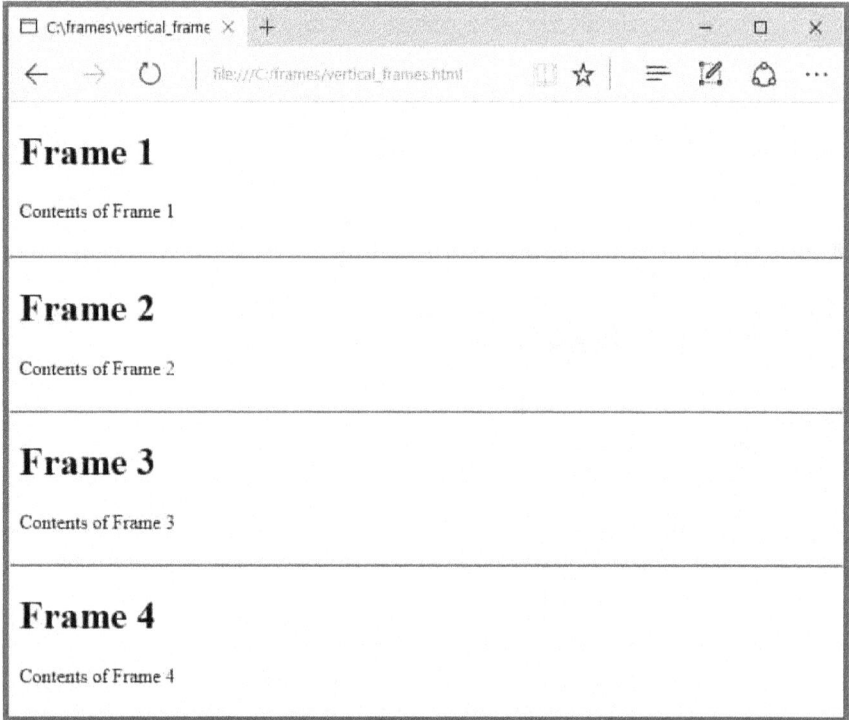

Combining Columns and Rows

You can have both rows and columns of frames on one web page and this is done by nesting a frameset inside another one. First, the frameset is created – this is the parent element. Then another is created inside it – this is the child frameset. The next example shows nesting two rows inside three columns:

```
<frameset cols="*,*,*">
```

```
<frameset rows="*,*">
    <frame src="frame_1.html">
    <frame src="frame_2.html">
</frameset>
<frame src="frame_3.html">
<frame src="frame_4.html">
</frameset>
```

And the result of that is:

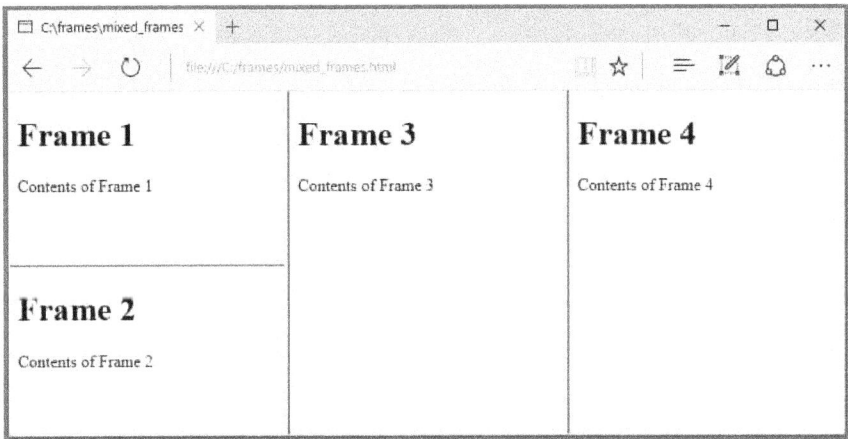

Note that the nested frameset is in the parent element in place of the first frame. Nested elements can go anywhere, for example, if we wanted in the center, we could simply do this:

```
<frameset cols="*,*,*">
    <frame src="frame_1.html">
    <frameset rows="*,*">
        <frame src="frame_2.html">
        <frame src="frame_3.html">
    </frameset>
    <frame src="frame_4.html">
</frameset>
```

193

And it would look like this:

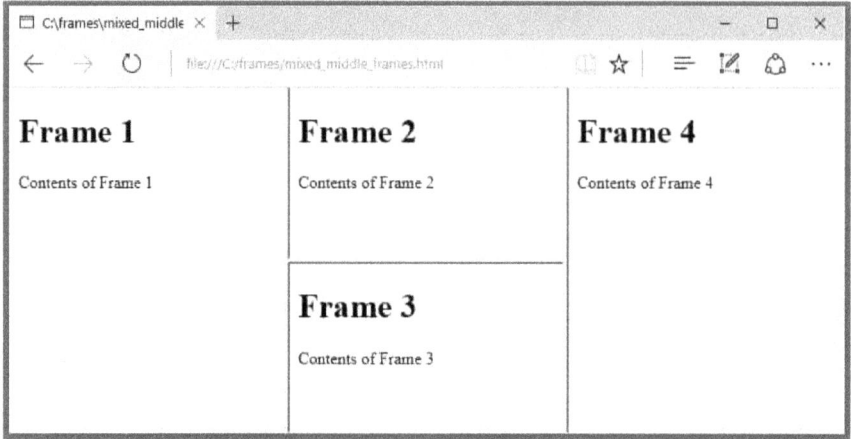

We can also have extra nested frames:

```
<frameset cols="*,*">
    <frame src="frame_1.html">
    <frameset rows="*,*">
        <frame src="frame_2.html">
        <frameset cols="*,*">
            <frame src="frame_3.html">
            <frame src="frame_4.html">
        </frameset>
    </frameset>
</frameset>
```

And that will give us two columns of the same size. The second is split between two rows, and the second row is split into a pair of columns:

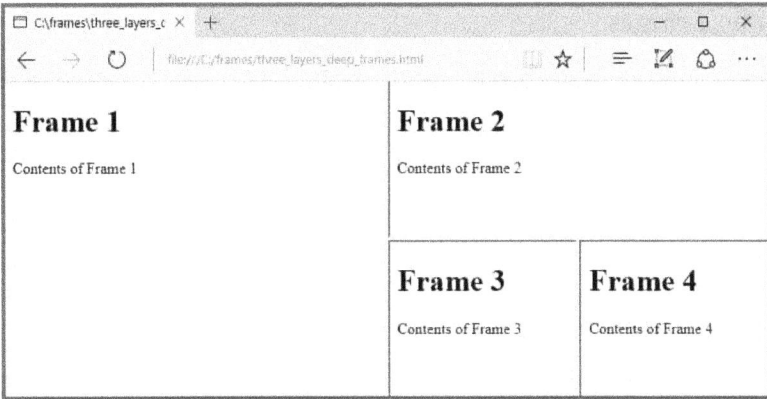

Another way of creating combinations of columns and rows is defining a grid in one frameset. For example, we could have four frames, equally sized:

```
<frameset rows="*,*" cols="*,*">
    <frame src="frame_1.html">
    <frame src="frame_2.html">
    <frame src="frame_3.html">
    <frame src="frame_4.html">
</frameset>
```

And that would look like this:

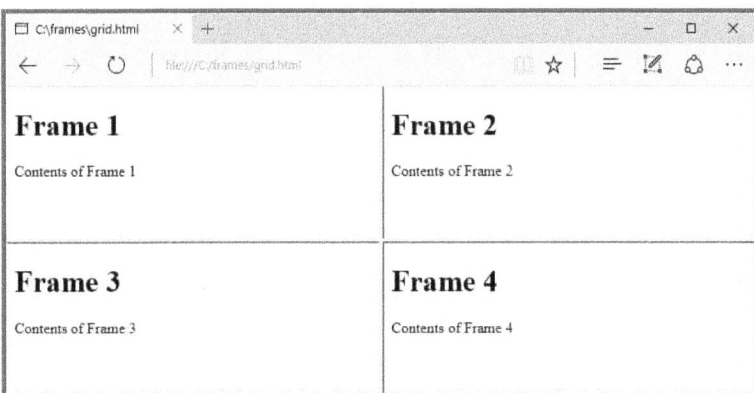

Styling Frames

When you style a web page with frames, you can use two styling types:

- Within the frame

- The entire frameset

When you style each individual frame, the definition must be done in the source document, while the frameset styling is done in the parent document that has the frameset.

Style and Format the Frameset

To change how a frameset is presented, you can do a few things:

- Specify and lock the size of the frame

- Change the margins between the frames

- Format the borders around the frames

Rather than using CSS, as you would expect, you can do this in HTML by giving the frame elements specific attributes and values.

Sizing the Frames

You can size a frame by percentages or pixels or set them, so they adjust automatically based on what space is available. Specifying the size requires the value to be inserted into the rows or cols attribute.

By default, any visitor to your website can use their mouse to resize the frames by dragging the border – unless you add the attribute, noresize, to the frame.

Let's how both of these work. We'll create a layout that has a full-width row at the top of the webpage and three columns beneath it – the first and third are sized to give us sidebars and the middle is a larger area for content:

```
<frameset rows="150px,*">
    <frame noresize src="frame_1.html">
    <frameset cols="20%,*,20%">
        <frame src="frame_2.html">
        <frame src="frame_3.html">
        <frame src="frame_4.html">
    </frameset>
</frameset>
```

This code creates a frameset containing two rows – the first is 150px tall, and it cannot be resized because we added the noresize attribute. The styles applied to frame_.html are still there but only for the specified frame's content, while the second row will expand, filling in whatever space is available.

In the second row, we nested another frameset with three columns. The first column and the third will each have 20% of the available window, while the second resizes automatically to take the rest of the space. Because the noresize attribute has not been used on the columns, initially, they will render based on what sizes the code specified, but website visitors will be able to resize them manually.

Here's what it looks like:

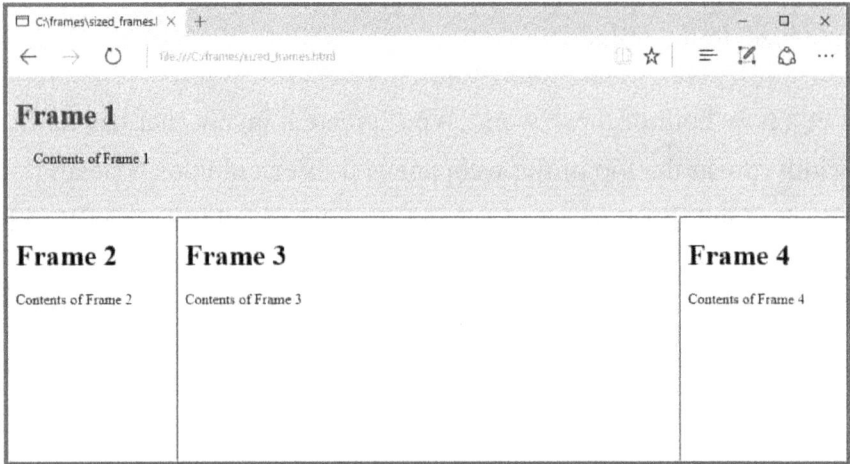

Format the Frame Margins and Borders

The layout is defined and the margins between frames can be resized. We can also get rid of the border between the frames. Using our previously created layout, we're going to remove the borders that go between the columns but leave the one that separates the top and bottom rows. We will also add a margin around the first frame's contents:

```
<frameset rows="150px,*">
    <frame noresize src="frame_1.html"
marginheight="15">
    <frameset cols="20%,*,20%">
        <frame src="frame_2.html"
frameborder="0">
        <frame src="frame_3.html"
frameborder="0">
        <frame src="frame_4.html"
frameborder="0">
    </frameset>
```

```
</frameset>
```

We applied a marginheight attribute to the first frames, giving a margin of 15px above the content and the below it. The frameborder has a value of 0, removing the borders from the three frames at the bottom.

Here's what it looks like:

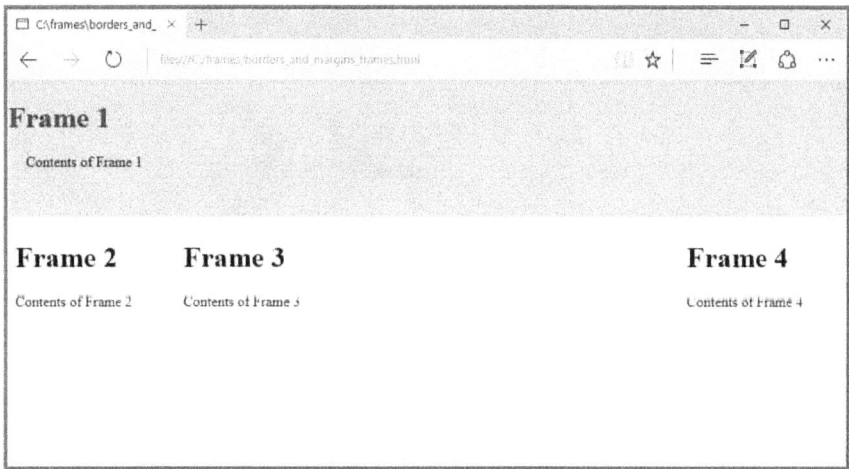

Using Links to Target Frames

One of the more common ways we use frames is to add sticky navigation to an always-visible frame, no matter what position the content holds in the other frames. When these are implemented correctly, navigation links will lead to new resources loading in a single frame while the remaining frames are static.

We can also format anchors, so they target particular frames, and this is done by assigning a targeted frame element with a name attribute and then using that attributed target in the <a> element – this will result in <href> being loaded in the targeted frame.

Does that sound clear to you? Let's look at it one step at a time.

First, a name must be assigned to the frame where we want our links to open. We'll use the layout we created in the last example – we'll make the left-hand column for the navigation, and the center column will be the targeted frame. To do this, the target needs a name assigned to it:

```
<frameset rows="150px,*">
    <frame noresize src="frame_1.html"
marginheight="15">
    <frameset cols="20%,*,20%">
        <frame src="frame_2.html"
frameborder="0">
        <frame src="frame_3.html"
name="mid_col" frameborder="0">
        <frame src="frame_4.html"
frameborder="0">
    </frameset>
</frameset>
```

The center column has been given the name, name="mid_col" so now some links can be created in the source document for the left column, called frame_2.html, and the center column targeted:

```
<!DOCTYPE html>
<html>
<body>
    <h1>Frame 2</h1>
    <p>Contents of Frame 2</p>
    <ul>
```

```
              <li><a href="frame_1.html"
    target="mid_col">Load frame_1.html</a></li>
              <li><a href="frame_2.html"
    target="mid_col">Load frame_2.html</a></li>
              <li><a href="frame_3.html"
    target="mid_col">Load frame_3.html</a></li>
              <li><a href="frame_4.html"
    target="mid_col">Load frame_4.html</a></li>
              </ul>
    </body>
    </html>
```

When the webpage loads, there are four links in the sidebar on the left. When a link is clicked, the relevant file contents show in the center column frame, attributed with name="mid_col".

When the page loads, this is what we see first:

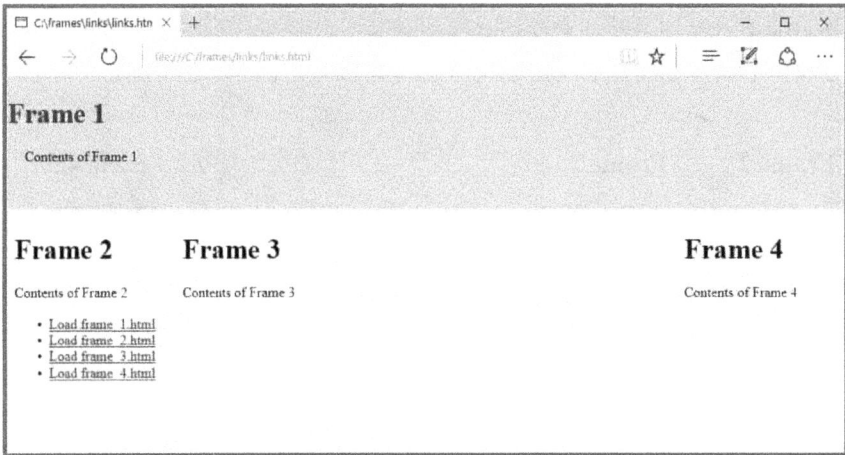

If Load Frame_1.html is clicked on, we would see the file contents load in the center column, like this:

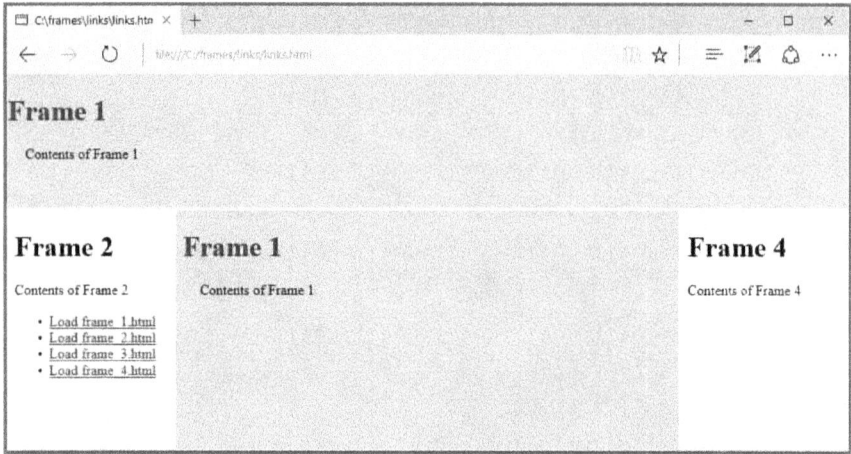

If Load frame_2.html is clicked, the navigation contents show in the center column and the left-hand sidebar:

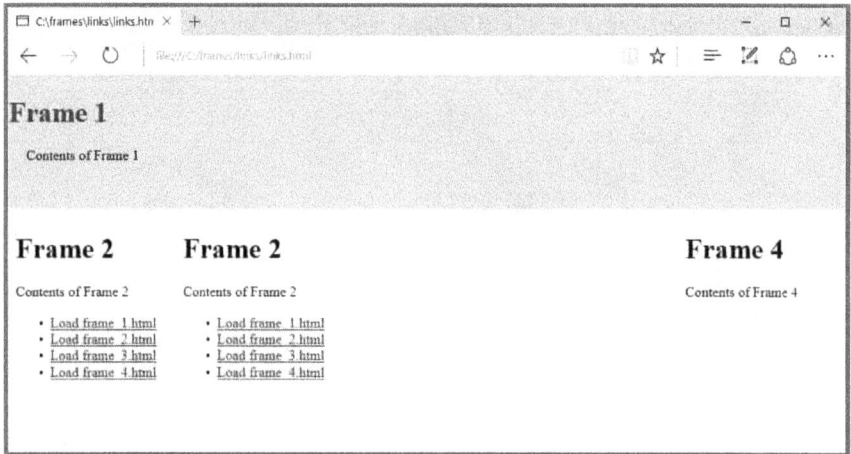

And when Load frame_3.html and Load frame_4.html are clicked, they do what you expect them to do – load the contents in the center column.

If we had omitted target="mid_col" from a link, it would show the resource load in the frame where the link is contained when that link is clicked. If we need the whole page reloaded, i.e., when an external website is linked to, target="_blank" or target="_top" needs to be added to the anchor element.

HTML iframes

Iframes are used for displaying nested web pages, which are web pages inside other web pages. The <iframe> tag is used for defining inline frames. An iframe will embed a document inside another HTML document, inside the rectangular region. However, JavaScript is required for the contents of the iframe and the web page to interact with one another.

Iframe Syntax

The syntax used to define HTML iframes is:

```
<iframe src="URL"></iframe>
```

The attribute, src, is used for specifying the inline frame page web address.

Setting the Height and Width

The width and height are set by using the attributes called width and height. However, values are in pixels by default, but you can set them to percentages.

Here's an example in pixels:

```
<!DOCTYPE html>
<html>
<body>
```

```
<h2>HTML Iframes example</h2>
<p> The height and width attributes specify
the iframe size:</p>
<iframe src="https://www.wikipedia.com/"
height="300" width="400"></iframe>
</body>
</html>
```

The output is:

HTML Iframes example

The height and width attributes specify the iframe size:

And another example using percentages:

```
<!DOCTYPE html>
<html>
<body>
<h2>HTML Iframes</h2>
<p> The height and width attributes specify
the iframe size:</p>
<iframe src="https://www.wikipedia.com/"
height="50%" width="70%"></iframe>
</body>
</html>
```

The output is:

HTML Iframes

The height and width attributes specify the iframe size:

It is also possible to change an iframe border's color, size and style:

```
<!DOCTYPE html>
```

```
<html>
<body>
<h2>Custom Iframe Border</h2>
<iframe src="https://www.wikipedia.com/"
style="border:2px solid tomato;"></iframe>
</body>
</html>
```

The output is

Custom Iframe Border

Followed by webpage surrounded in a red border.

Using an iframe Target as a Link

An iframe can be used to set a target frame as a link. The link's target attribute must refer to the iframe's name attribute:

```
<!DOCTYPE html>
<html>
<body>

<h2>Iframe - Target for a Link</h2>
<iframe height="300px" width="100%"
src="new.html" name="iframe_a"></iframe>
<p><a href="https://www.wikipedia.com"
target="iframe_a">Wikipedia.com</a></p>
<p>The iframe and link target name must have
the same value otherwise the link cannot
open as a frame. </p>

</body>
</html>
```

new.hmtl output code:

```
<!DOCTYPE html>
<html>
<head>
    <style>

    p{ font-size: 50px;
        color: red;}
</style>
</head>
<body style="background-color: #c7f15e;">
  <p>This is a link below the iframe click
on the link to open a new iframe. </p>
</body>
</html>
```

The output is:

Iframe – Target for a Link

This is a link below the iframe click on the link to open a new iframe

Wikipedia.com

The iframe and link target name must have the same value; otherwise, the link cannot open as a frame

Using Iframes to Embed YouTube Videos

The <iframe> tag can also be used to add a YouTube video to your web page. The video will play on the page, and you can set video properties, such as height, width, autoplay, and so on.

1. Find the YouTube video you want to be embedded

2. Under the video, click the Share button

3. Click on the Embed<> option

4. Copy the HTML code and paste it to your file

5. Change the properties as you need to.

Here's an example:

```
<iframe width="550" height="315"
src="https://www.whatever video you choose"
frameborder="0" allow="accelerometer;
autoplay; encrypted-media; gyroscope;
picture-in-picture" allowfullscreen
style="padding:20px;"></iframe>
        <iframe width="550" height="315"
src="https://www.youtube.com/embed/O5hShUO6w
xq" frameborder="0" allow="accelerometer;
autoplay; encrypted-media; gyroscope;
picture-in-picture"
style="padding:20px;">></iframe>
```

Input a YouTube link and the run the code – you should see your video playing.

Iframe Attributes

These are the <iframe> attributes

Attribute Name	Value	Description
allowfullscreen	Pixels	If this is set to true, the frame may open in full-screen mode

height	Pixels	This defines the embedded iframe's height – 150 px is the default
name	text	This gives the iframe the name. this is an important attribute if you want a link created in one frame
frameborder	1 or 0	This defines whether a border should be added - HTML5 does not support this
Width	Pixels	This defines the embedded iframe's width – 300 px is the default
src	URL	This attribute provides the path or file name of the content to be loaded into the iframe
sandbox		This is used for applying additional restrictions for the frame contents

	allow-forms	This allows the form to be submitted. The form will not be submitted if this keyword is not used
	allow-popups	This enables popups if applied – if not, no popups are enabled
	allow-scripts	This enables the script to run
	allow-same-origin	This allows the embedded resource to be treated as though downloaded from the same source
srcdoc		This attribute allows the HTML content to be shown in the inline frame, overriding src, provided the browser supports it
scrolling		This attribute indicates to the browser that a scroll bar should or should not

		be provided for the iframe – this is NOT supported in HTML5
	auto	This shows the scrollbar only if the iframe's content is bigger than the iframe's dimensions
	yes	The iframe scrollbar will always be shown
	no	The iframe scrollbar will never be shown

Chapter 9

HTML Comments and File Paths

HTML Comments

In computer coding, comments are text or code written to explain to the coder and others who read it what the code does. The user does not see them and, provided they are added properly, the compiler will ignore them.

Comments can be added in HTML by using the <!-- ... --> tag – anything written in this tag is treated as a comment:

The syntax"

```
<! -- Write your commented text here -->
```

For example:

```
<!--   <p>Here is some text</p>
<p>Here is more text</p> -->
```

Here's a full example::

```
<!DOCTYPE html>
<html>
```

```
<!-- This is the Header section -->
<head>
    <!-- Internal CSS -->
    <style>
        body{
            text-align: center;
            background-color: #f0f8ff;
            font-size: 30px;
            color: red;
        }
    </style>
</head>

<!-- This is the body section, code you want
displayed on the web page should be written
here -->
<body>
    <!-- heading tag -->
 <h2>First Web Page</h2>

 <!-- Paragraph tag -->
 <p>Write your Content here!!!</p>
</body>
</html>
```

The output is:

First Web Page

Write your Content here!!!

Multiline Comments

HTML code also allows for multiline comments, where you can add code descriptions, debugging instructions, and so on. Here's the syntax:

```
<!---

Your code is commented.

Write a description of the code.

It will not be displayed on the web page.

-->
```

Here's an example:

```
<h2>Cake Gallery</h2>
<!-- This is an image for a scrumptious cake
you can see the image on the web page
in your favorite browser -->
<img
src="https://static.xxxxx.com/htmlpages/imag
es/cake.png" alt="cake image" height="300px"
 width="300px">
```

(please note that xxxxx.com is in place of a real website or image source)

The output is:

HTML File Paths

HTML file paths describe where a file is within a folder on the website. They are much like the addresses you type into a web browser to find a specific website. Any external resource can be linked into the HTML file, using file paths like images, JS files, CSS files, videos, and so on.

The <href> and <src> attributes need an attribute when they are to link the HTML file to an external source.

These are the different ways a file path may be specified:

- **<img src="picture.jpg">** - this is used to specify that picture.jpg is in the same folder that the current page is in.

- **<img src="images/picture.jpg">** - this is used to specify that picture.jpg is in the current folder, in another folder called "images".

- **<img src="/images/picture.jpg">** - this is used to specify that picture.jpg is in the current web's root, in the "images" folder.

- **<img src="../picture.jpg">** - this is used to specify that picture.jpg is in a folder one level above the current one.

We use file paths on our web pages for linking the following kinds of external file:

- Images

- JavaScript

- Style sheets

- Web pages

There are also two types of file path – absolute and relative.

Absolute File Paths

These are used to specify a full URL address, for example:

```
<!DOCTYPE html>
<html>
<body>
<h2>Using a Full URL File Path</h2>
```

```
<img
src="https://www.xxxxx.com/images/nature-
1.jpg" alt="image" style="width:300px">
</body>
</html>
```

The output would be:

Using an Absolute File Path

Relative File Paths

Relative file paths specify files related to the current page's location. In this example, we'll look at how a file path can be used to point to a file located in "images" at the current web's root:

```
<!DOCTYPE html>
<html>
<body>
<h2>Using a Relative File Path</h2>
<img src="/images/nature-2.jpg"
alt="Mountain" style="width:300px">
</body>
</html>
```

The output is:

Using a Relative File Path

And in this example, how a file path can be used to point to a file in the current folder, in another folder called "images"

```
<!DOCTYPE html>
<html>
<body>
<h2>Using a Relative File Path</h2>
<img src="images/nature-3.jpg"
alt="Mountain" style="width:300px">
</body>
</html>
```

The output is:

Using a Relative File Path

This example shows how a file path can be used to point to a file in the folder one above the current one:

```
<!DOCTYPE html>
<html>
<body>
<h2>Using a Relative File Path</h2>
<img src="../images/nature4.jpg"
alt="Mountain" style="width:300px">
</body>
</html>
```

The output is:

Using a Relative File Path

Important Points

- Always use the correct file name, URL, image name, and so on. Otherwise it cannot be displayed on the web page

- Relative file paths are better, ensuring your code is not dependent on URLs.

Chapter 10

The HTML Head

The <head> tag in HTML is used to hold metadata, which is data about the data, and it goes between the <html> and <body> tags. The content in the HTML head is not shown on the web page by the browser. It simply contains metadata about the document, which, in turn, is specifying data relating to the HTML document.

How much metadata the HTML head contains is dependent on what we require – it can have a lot, of it can have a little. However, it is a critical part of the document when you are creating your website.

The metadata can be used to define the title of the document, the character set, the links, styles, scripts and so on. These are the tags that may be used in the metadata:

- <title>

- <style>

- <meta>

- <link>

- <script>

- <base>

HTML <title> Element

We use the <title> element for defining the document title. This is used in all HTML and XHTML documents and must be between the <head> tags. A document may have only one title element.

The <title> element:

- Defines the title as seen in the browser tab

- Provides a page title when it is placed into favorites

- Displays a page title in search engine results

Note - this element must contain specific information about the document, and the recommended length is 65 to 70 spaces – that includes spaces.

Here's an example:

```
<!DOCTYPE html>
<html>
<head>
<title>The Page Title</title>
</head>
<body>
<p>The content in the body is shown in the
browser window.</p>
```

```
<p>The title element content is shown in the
browser tab, in the search engine results
and in  favorites.</p>
</body>
</html>
```

The output is:

The content in the body is shown in the browser window.

The title element content is shown in the browser tab, search engine results, and favorites.

HTML <style> Element

This is used for styling your HTML page. Although CSS is not in the scope of this book, it is worth noting that the <style> element may contain CSS properties ONLY for that specific HTML page. Here's an example:

```
<!DOCTYPE html>
<html>
<head>
<title>This is the Page Title</title>
<style>
body {background-color: pink;}
h1 {color: red;}
p {color: blue;}
</style>
</head>
<body>
<h1>This is a Heading</h1>
<p>This is a paragraph.</p>
</body>
</html>
```

The output is:

This is a Heading

This is a paragraph.

HTML <link> Element

The <link> element is used when you want external stylesheets linked to your web page. It has two attributes – "rel" and "href". "rel" is used to say that it is a stylesheet, while "href" provides the path leading to the file. Here's the example:

```
<!DOCTYPE html>
<html>
<head>
<title>This is the title</title>
<link rel="stylesheet" href="style.css">
</head>
<body>
<h2>Web page with external CSS</h2>
<p>This looks cool</p>
</body>
</html>
```

The output is:

Web page with external CSS

This is looks cool

HTML <meta> Element

We use the <meta> element when we want the character set specified, along with the page description, the authors, keywords, and any other page metadata. Typically, search engines, browsers, and other web services use the metadata as a way of giving your web page a better ranking.

Let's look at how metadata is used.

Defining a character set:

```
<meta charset="UTF-8">
```

The charset attribute is used to specify the encoding for the character. In this example, we are using "UTF-8", meaning any language can be displayed. Here's the example:

```
<!DOCTYPE html>
<html>
<head>
<meta charset="UTF-8">
</head>
<body>
<p>This is written in English  <span
style="color: blue"> My friend's name
is.......</span></p>
<p>This is Chinese language <span
style="color: red">Wǒ de péngyǒu
jiào</span></p>
</body>
</html>
```

The output is:

This is written in English. My friend's name is.......

This is Chinese language W? de péngy?u jiào

Defining your web page description:

```
<meta name="description" content="Free Web
tutorials">
```

Meta descriptions are useful for search engines to known what to look for.

Defining search engine keywords:

```
<meta name="keywords" content="HTML, CSS,
XML, JavaScript">
```

Keyword values are also used when you need to provide a search engine with keywords, but, thanks largely to spammers, the browser may ignore it.

Defining the webpage author:

```
<meta name="author" content="Akon">
```

This value is used to specify who writes the content on the web page and some content management systems use it to automatically extract the author details.

Refreshing documents every 30 seconds:

```
<meta http-equiv="refresh" content="30">
```

Meta refresh tells the browser to refresh the page automatically after the specified time. We set it to refresh after 30 seconds but you can set it for whatever time period you require.

```
<meta http-equiv="refresh" content="10;
url=https://www.Wikipedia.com/
```

If a URL that has content value is added, that page is redirected to once the set time is over. Here's an example:

```
<!DOCTYPE html>
<html>
<head>
<meta http-equiv="refresh" content="5;
url=https://www.Wikipedia.com/ ">
</head>
<body>
<h2>Meta element Example</h2>
<p style="color: green;">Please wait for 5
seconds and it will automatically redirect
to the URL specified in meta tag</p>
</body>
</html>
```

The output is:

Meta element Example

Please wait for 5 seconds and it will automatically redirect to the URL specified in meta tag

Here is an example that shows all the meta elements used in the head:

```
<!DOCTYPE html>
<html>
<head>
<meta charset="UTF-8">
<meta name="description" content="Free Web
tutorials">
<meta name="keywords"
content="HTML,CSS,XML,JavaScript">
<meta name="author" content="Akon">
</head>
<body>
<p>All the meta information are set.</p>
</body>
</html>
```

The output is:

This is written in English. My friend's name is.......

This is Chinese language W? de péngy?u jiào

Using the <meta> tag to set the Viewport

This was introduced into HTML5 and is used to control the viewport, the area that a user sees on the web page. It is different depending on what device is being used and, obviously, is much smaller on a mobile device than a computer screen.

The syntax is:

```
<meta name="viewport" content="width=device-
width, initial-scale=1.0">
```

The <meta> viewport tag is used to specify how the scaling and dimensions are controlled on the page:

- **width=device-width** – this is used to set the page width to follow the width of the screen the user is viewing the page on.

- **initial-scale=1.0** – this sets the initial level of zoom when the browser first loads the page.

Here's an example without using the viewport <meta> tag:

```
<!DOCTYPE html>
<html>
<body>

<p><b>Understanding this example requires
that you open the page on a mobile
device.</b></p>

<img src="image.jpg" alt="image" width="460"
height="345">

<p>
```

Lorem ipsum dolor sit amet, consectetuer adipiscing elit, sed diam nonummy nibh euismod tincidunt ut

laoreet dolore magna aliquam erat volutpat. Ut wisi enim ad minim veniam, quis nostrud exerci tation

ullamcorper suscipit lobortis nisl ut aliquip ex ea commodo consequat. Duis autem vel

eum iriure dolor in hendrerit in vulputate velit esse molestie consequat, vel illum dolore eu feugiat nulla facilisis at vero eros et accumsan et iusto odio dignissim qui blandit praesent luptatum

zzril delenit augue duis dolore te feugait nulla facilisi. Nam liber tempor cum soluta nobis

eleifend option congue nihil imperdiet doming id quod mazim placerat facer possim assum.

Nam liber tempor cum soluta nobis eleifend option congue nihil imperdiet doming id quod mazim placerat

facer possim assum.

```
        </p>

    </body>
    </html>
```

The output is:

Understanding this example requires that you open the page on a mobile device.

Lorem ipsum dolor sit amet, consectetuer adipiscing elit, sed diam nonummy nibh euismod tincidunt ut laoreet dolore magna aliquam erat volutpat. Ut wisi enim ad minim veniam, quis nostrud exerci tation ullamcorper suscipit lobortis nisl ut aliquip ex ea commodo consequat. Duis autem vel eum iriure dolor in hendrerit in vulputate velit esse molestie consequat, vel illum dolore eu feugiat nulla facilisis at vero eros et accumsan et iusto odio dignissim qui blandit praesent luptatum zzril delenit augue duis dolore te feugait nulla facilisi. Nam liber tempor cum soluta nobis eleifend option congue nihil imperdiet doming id quod mazim placerat facer possim assum. Nam liber tempor cum soluta nobis eleifend option congue nihil imperdiet doming id quod mazim placerat facer possim assum.

This is with the viewport <meta> tag:

```
<!DOCTYPE html>
<html>
<head>
<meta name="viewport" content="width=device-width, initial-scale=1.0"/>
<style>
img {
    max-width: 100%;
    height: auto;
}
</style>
</head>
<body>
<p><b>Understanding this example requires you to open the page on a mobile device.</b></p>

<img src="image.jpg" alt="image" width="460" height="345">

<p>
```

Lorem ipsum dolor sit amet, consectetuer adipiscing elit, sed diam nonummy nibh euismod tincidunt ut

laoreet dolore magna aliquam erat volutpat. Ut wisi enim ad minim veniam, quis nostrud exerci tation ullamcorper suscipit lobortis nisl ut aliquip ex ea commodo consequat. Duis autem vel

eum iriure dolor in hendrerit in vulputate velit esse molestie consequat, vel illum dolore eu

feugiat nulla facilisis at vero eros et accumsan et iusto odio dignissim qui blandit praesent luptatum

zzril delenit augue duis dolore te feugait nulla facilisi. Nam liber tempor cum soluta nobis

eleifend option congue nihil imperdiet doming id quod mazim placerat facer possim assum.

Nam liber tempor cum soluta nobis eleifend option congue nihil imperdiet doming id quod mazim placerat

facer possim assum.

```
        </p>

    </body>
</html>
```

The output is:

Understanding this example requires you to open the page on a mobile device.

Lorem ipsum dolor sit amet, consectetuer adipiscing elit, sed diam nonummy nibh euismod tincidunt ut laoreet dolore magna aliquam erat volutpat. Ut wisi enim ad minim veniam, quis nostrud exerci tation ullamcorper suscipit lobortis nisl ut aliquip ex ea commodo consequat. Duis autem vel eum iriure dolor in hendrerit in vulputate velit esse molestie consequat, vel illum dolore eu feugiat nulla facilisis at vero eros et accumsan et iusto odio dignissim qui blandit praesent luptatum zzril delenit augue duis dolore te feugait nulla facilisi. Nam liber tempor cum soluta nobis eleifend option congue nihil imperdiet doming id quod mazim placerat facer possim assum. Nam liber tempor cum soluta nobis eleifend option congue nihil imperdiet doming id quod mazim placerat facer possim assum.

Note – to clearly see the difference, you should open both of these previous examples on a mobile device.

HTML <base> Element

The <base> element specifies the base URL and target for every relative URL on the page:

```
<!DOCTYPE html>
<html>
<head>
<title>Page Title</title>
<base href="https://static.Wikipedia.com/
/images/" target="_blank">
</head>
<body>
<img src="html5.png">
<p>The base URL has been specified and the
browser will look for the image "html5.png"
at
"https://static.Wikipedia.com/htmlpages/imag
es/html5.png"</p>
```

```
<p><a href="
https://www.Wikipedia.com">Wikipedia</a></p>
<p>This link opens in a new window as the
base target has been set to "_blank".</p>
</body>
</html>
```

The output is:

The base URL has been specified, and the browser will look for the image "html5.png at "https://static.Wikipedia.com/ /images/html5.png"

Wikipedia

This link opens in a new window as the base target has been set to "_blank".

Chapter 11

HTML Layout

HTML layouts are how we arrange our web pages in a well-structured and responsive manner. It is one of the most important aspects of creating a website to keep in mind; a great layout ensures your website looks professional and the content is laid out in the most appropriate and user-friendly way.

These are the HTML5 elements you can use to define parts of your web page:

- **<header>:** Used for defining a section or document's header.

- **<nav>:** Used for defining containers to hold navigation links.

- **<section>:** Used for defining document sections.

- **<article>:** Used for defining self-contained, independent articles.

- **<aside>**: Used for defining content beside content, such as sidebars.

- **<footer>**: Used for defining section or document footers.

- **<details>**: Used for defining extra details.

- **<summary>**: Used the <details> element headings.

HTML layouts ensure that each part of the web page has its own properly created space and can be arranged in the right order.

Layout Elements

These delve into the elements listed above:

HTML <header>

This element is used when you want your web page header sections created. Here, you include the heading element, the introductory content, webpage icon or logo and information about the author. Here's an example:

```
<header style="background-color: #303030;
height: 80px; width: 100%">
     <h1 style="font-size: 30px; color:
white;text-align: center; padding-top:
15px;">Welcome to     MyFirstWebpage</h1>
  </header>
```

The output is:

My First Webpage

HTML <nav>

This is a container where the main navigation links go and these links can be for the same page or external. Here's an example:

```
<nav style="background-color:#bcdeef;">
        <h1 style="text-align:
center;">Navigation Links</h1>
        <ul>
            <li><a href="#">link1</a></li>
            <li><a href="#">link2</a></li>
            <li><a href="#">link3</a></li>
            <li><a href="#">link4</a></li>
        </ul>
    </nav>
```

The output is:

Navigation Links

- link1

- link2

- link3

- link4

HTML <section>

The <section> elements are used for separate sections where related elements are placed together. These sections can contain images, text, videos, tables, and so on. Here's an example:

```
<section style="background-color:#ff7f50; width: 100%; border:
1px solid black;">
```

```
    <h2>Introduction to HTML</h2>
    <p>HTML is a markup language used to
create nice web pages with styling, and
looks nice on a web browser..</p>
    </section>
```

The output is:

```
Introduction to HTML
```

HTML is a markup language used to create nice web pages with styling, and looks nice on a web browser.

HTML <article>

The <article> tag is used when you want a self-contained article contained. This includes large articles, huge stories and so on.

```
<article style="width: 100%; border:2px
solid black; background-color: #fff0f5;">
    <h2>History of the World</h2>
    <p>Write your content here for the
history of the world</p>
</article>
```

The output is:

History of the World

Write your content here for the history of the world

HTML <aside>

This element is used for defining aside content that is related to the web page's primary contact, such as in a side bar.

```
<aside style="background-color:#e6e6fa">
    <h2>Sidebar information</h2>
    <p>This contains information represented
on the web page as a sidebar.</p>
  </aside>
```

The output is:

Sidebar information

This contains information represented on the web page as a sidebar

HTML <footer>

The <footer> element is used for defining the footer for the specified web page or document and mostly has information about copyright, the author and other relevant links.

```
<footer style="background-color: #f0f8ff;
width: 100%; text-align: center;">
    <h3>Footer Example</h3>
    <p>© Copyright 2018-2020. </p>
</footer>
```

The output is:

```
Footer Example
© Copyright 2018-2020.
```

HTML \<details\>

This element is used when you want additional details added about the page and these details can be shown or hidden as needed. Here's an example:

```
<details style="background-color: #f5deb3">
    <summary>This is visible : click to show
other details</summary>
    <p>This section only shows when the user
wants to see it. </p>
 </details>
```

The output is:

> This is visible : click to show other details.
>
> This section only shows **when the user wants** to see it

HTML \<summary\>

The last element is \<summary\> and this is used with the \<details\> element. It shows summaries or captions about the content in \<details\>.

```
<details>
    <summary>HTML is an acronym
for?</summary>
    <p style="color: blue; font-size:
20px;">Hypertext Markup Language</p>
 </details>
```

The output is:

> HTML is acronym for?

Chapter 12

HTML Entities, Symbols and Charset

HTML Entities

In HTML, character entities are used to replace reserved characters and those that do not appear on your keyboard. These entities provide us with many characters that we can use to add mathematical operators, geometric shapes, icons, and so on.

For example, if the greater than (>) or less than (<) symbols are used in your text, the browser may confuse them with being tags. So, we use character entities to take their place.

How to Use Entities

Entities can be used by name or using a numerical reference. Each one begins with the & (ampersand symbol) and ends with the ; (semicolon). Here's the syntax:

```
&entity_name;
   OR
&#entity_number;
```

The following table shows you the most common character entities in HTML:

Result	Description	Entity Name	Entity Number
	Non-breaking space		160
<	Less than	&lt;	60
>	Greater than	&gt;	62
&	Ampersand	&amp;	38
"	Double quotation mark	&quot;	34
'	Single quotation mark (apostrophe)	&apos;	39
¢	cent	&cent;	162
¢	cent	&cent;	162
£	pound	&pound;	163
¥	yen	&yen;	165
€	Euro	&euro;	8364
©	copyright	&copy;	169

Be aware that case sensitivity is important when using entity names.

The advantage of using entity names is that they are easy to remember, but you should be aware that browsers may not support every name – that said, they do tend to support the entity numbers.

Here's an example:

```
<!DOCTYPE html>
<html>
<head>
<title></title>
</head>
 <body>
    <h3>HTML entity example</h3>
    <p> "This is the content written in the
entity"</p>
    <p> <p> Paragraph tag </p>
 </body>
</html>
```

The output is:

HTML entity example

"This is the content written in the entity"

Paragraph tag

Diacritical Marks

In HTML, some special letter types have a glyph added below or above the letters – the glyphs are known as diacritical marks. Some of these diacritical marks, such as acute (´) and grave (`), are also known as accents. Diacritical marks may be used below, above, inside, and between letters.

These are the commonly used diacritical marks:

Mark	Character	Construct	Result
`	a	à	à
´	a	á	á
^	a	â	â
~	a	ã	ã
`	O	Ò	Ò
´	O	Ó	Ó
^	O	Ô	Ô
~	O	Õ	Õ

HTML Symbols

Many of the technical, mathematical, and currency symbols we use a lot are not always found on a keyboard. Instead, entity names are used to add these symbols to a page in HTML. If you cannot find the entity name or one does not exist, you can use a decimal or hexadecimal reference or entity number.

Here's an example:

```
<!DOCTYPE html>
    <html>
     <body>
        <h3> Currency Symbols</h3>
                <p>This is the Indian
Rupee symbol <b>₹<b></p>
            <p>This is the Euro symbol
<b>€</b></p>
            <p> This is the Dollar symbol
<b>#36;</b></p>
         </body>
       </html>
```

The output is:

Currency Symbols

This is the Indian Rupee symbol **?**

This is the Euro symbol **?**

This is the Dollar symbol **$**

These are the mathematical symbols HTML supports:

Char	Number	Entity	Description
∀	∀	∀	For All

Char	Number	Entity	Description
∂	∂	∂	Partial Differential
∃	∃	∃	There Exists
∅	∅	∅	Empty Sets
∇	∇	∇	Nabla
∈	∈	∈	Element Of
∉	∉	∉	Not An Element Of
∋	∋	∋	Contains As Member
∏	∏	∏	N-Ary Product
∑	∑	∑	N-Ary Summation

HTML also supports Greek Symbols:

Char	Number	Entity	Description*
Α	Α	Α	Greek Letter Alpha
Β	Β	Β	Greek Letter

			Beta
Γ	&#915;	&Gamma;	Greek Letter Gamma
Δ	&#916;	&Delta;	Greek Letter Delta
E	&#917;	&Epsilon;	Greek Letter Epsilon
Z	&#918;	&Zeta;	Greek Letter Zeta

* All these Greek letters are the capital letter versions.

Lastly, these are some of the more important HTML symbols:

Char	Number	Entity	Description
©	&#169;	&copy;	Copyright sign
®	&#174;	&reg;	Registered sign
€	&#8364;	&euro;	Euro sign
™	&#8482;	&trade;	Trademark
←	&#8592;	&larr;	Leftwards arrow

↑	&#8593;	&uarr;	Upwards arrow
→	&#8594;	&rarr;	Rightwards arrow
↓	&#8595;	&darr;	Downwards arrow
♠	&#9824;	&spades;	Black spade suit
♣	&#9827;	&clubs;	Black club suit
♥	&#9829;	&hearts;	Black heart suit
♦	&#9830;	&diams;	Black diamond suit

HTML Charset

To finish this chapter off, we'll talk briefly about the HTML charset. This refers to character sets or encoding and is used for displaying pages correctly. For a browser to display pages correctly, it must be told which encoding or character set is to be used.

There are several types of encoding:

ASCII Character Set

ASCII stands for American Standard Code for Information Interchange. In HTML, the first-ever character encoding standard is the ASCII standard. ASCII provides 128 different alphanumeric characters that could be used on the internet: numbers (0-9), English letters (A-Z), and some special characters like! $ + - ( ) @ <> . However, compared to other character sets, it is pretty limited.

ANSI Character Set

ANSI is an acronym for American National Standard Institute and is an extended version of ASCII with support for 256 characters. It is also known as Windows-1252 and, up to Windows 95, it was the default Windows set.

ISO-8859-1 Character Set

This was used as the default encoding in HTML 2.0 and is also an ASCII extension, including the support of international characters. Characters were also shown using full bytes, which means 8-bit.

UTF-8 Character Set

This is a variable width character set, covering virtually all the symbols and characters in the world. It is now the standard for HTML and is used because the others are somewhat limited in their support.

The UTF-8 syntax for HTML4 is:

```
<meta http-equiv="Content-Type"
content="text/html;charset=ISO-8859-1">
```

248

And for HTML5:

```
<meta charset="UTF-8">
```

Chapter 13

HTML Backgrounds, Colors, and Fonts

HTML Backgrounds

The default color of any web page is white, but HTML has you covered with two ways to change the background – using colors or images - if you don't like it.

We can look at both ways with examples to show you how they work.

HTML Background with Colors

The background of an HTML element, such as table and page body backgrounds, is controlled using the bgcolor attribute – this does not work in HTML5.)

The following syntax can be used with any HTML tag:

```
<tagname bgcolor = "color_value"...>
```

And color_value can be in any of these formats:

```
<!-- Format 1 - Use color name -->
<table bgcolor = "lime" >
```

```
<!-- Format 2 - Use hex value -->
<table bgcolor = "#f1f1f1" >

<!-- Format 3 - Use color value in RGB terms
-->
<table bgcolor = "rgb(0,0,120)" >
```

Here's an example showing how to set a tag background:

```
<!DOCTYPE html>
<html>

    <head>
        <title>HTML Background Colors</title>
    </head>

    <body>
        <!-- Format 1 - Use color name -->
        <table bgcolor = "yellow" width =
"100%">
            <tr>
                <td>
                    This background is yellow
                </td>
            </tr>
        </table>

        <!-- Format 2 - Use hex value -->
        <table bgcolor = "#6666FF" width =
"100%">
            <tr>
                <td>
                    This background is sky blue
                </td>
            </tr>
```

```
            </table>

            <!-- Format 3 - Use color value in RGB
     terms -->
            <table bgcolor = "rgb(255,0,255)"
     width = "100%">
               <tr>
                 <td>
                    This background is green
                 </td>
               </tr>
            </table>
        </body>

    </html>
```

This will produce this result:

```
This background is yellow
This background is sky blue
This background is green
```

Html Background with Images

We can also use the background attribute for controlling element backgrounds too, specifically tables and page bodies. Instead of a color, an image can be set as the background:

This syntax can be used with any HTML tag:

```
<tagname background = "Image URL"...>
```

The common formats are GIF, JPEG, and PNG.

Here's an example showing how the background of a table can be set to an image. Here, I would suggest that you insert your own image in the right place and see how it turns out on your computer:

```
<!DOCTYPE html>
<html>

    <head>
        <title>HTML Background Images</title>
    </head>

    <body>
        <!-- Set table background -->
        <table background = "/images/html.gif"
width = "100%" height = "100">
            <tr><td>
                This background is filled up
with HTML image.
            </td></tr>
        </table>
    </body>

</html>
```

The output is:

```
This background is filled up with HTML
image.
```

Patterned and Transparent Backgrounds

On some websites, you can see that the background is patterned or transparent, and this is easily achievable by using a patterned or transparent image. When you use PNG or GIF images to do this, try

253

to use the smallest possible dimensions, even down to 1x1, as this will prevent slow loading.

Here's an example – again, use your own image for this:

```html
<!DOCTYPE html>
<html>

    <head>
        <title>HTML Background Images</title>
    </head>

    <body>
        <!-- Set a table background using a
pattern -->
        <table background =
"/images/pattern1.gif" width = "100%" height
= "100">
            <tr>
                <td>
                    This background has a pattern
image.
                </td>
            </tr>
        </table>

        <!-- Another example of a pattern used
as a table background -->
        <table background =
"/images/pattern2.gif" width = "100%" height
= "100">
            <tr>
                <td>
                    This background has a pattern
image.
                </td>
```

```
        </tr>
      </table>
    </body>

  </html>
```

The output is:

```
This background has a pattern image.
This background has a pattern image.
```

HTML Colors

Colors are one of the most important ways of providing your web pages with a great look and feel. Each page can have its own color specified using the <body> tag, or you can use the bgcolor attribute to set a color for an individual tag.

The <body> tag can have the following attributes:

- **bgcolor** – used to set the page background color.

- **text** – used to set the body text color.

- **alink** – used to set the link color for active or selected links.

- **link** – used to set the linked text color.

- **vlink** – used to set the color of the visited links, i.e., for links that have already been clicked on.

Color Coding Methods

You can use these three methods to set your web page colors:

- **Color names** – the color name can be directly specified, such as green, red, blue, etc.

- **Hex codes** – you can use a 6-digit number that represents the color made up of set amounts of red, green, and blue.

- **Color decimal or percentage values** – the rgb() property is used to set the value.

Let's look at these in turn:

Color Names

The color can be directly specified using the color name to set your background or text color. There are 16 basic names that can be validated using an HTML validator but, overall, more than 200 different names are supported by the biggest browsers.

These are the standard colors:

	Black		Gray		Silver		White
	Yellow		Lime		Aqua		Fuchsia
	Red		Green		Blue		Purple
	Maroon		Olive		Navy		Teal

Here's an example showing how to use this method to set a tag's background color:

```html
<!DOCTYPE html>
<html>

    <head>
        <title>HTML Colors by Name</title>
    </head>

    <body text = "blue" bgcolor = "green">
        <p>Use different colors for the body
and table  and see what the result is.</p>

        <table bgcolor = "black">
            <tr>
                <td>
                    <font color = "white">This
text will be shown as white on black
background.</font>
                </td>
            </tr>
        </table>
    </body>

</html>
```

The output is:

Use different colors for the body and table and see what the result is.

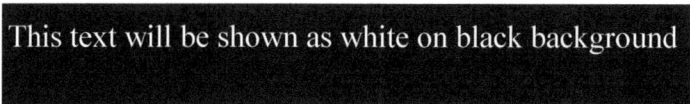
This text will be shown as white on black background

Hex Codes

Hexadecimals are 6-digit color representations. The first two are RR, representing red, the second two are GG, representing green, and the third two are BB, representing blue.

Hexadecimal values can come from MS Paint, Paintshop Pro, Adobe Photoshop, and many other similar graphics software.

Each code has a hash (#) or pound (£) sign in front of it. These are some of the colors that use a hexadecimal notation:

Color	Color HEX
	#000000
	#FF0000
	#00FF00
	#0000FF
	#FFFF00
	#00FFFF
	#FF00FF

	#C0C0C0
	#FFFFFF

Here's an example showing how hexadecimal values are used to set a tag's background:

```
<!DOCTYPE html>
<html>

    <head>
        <title>HTML Colors by Hex</title>
    </head>

    <body text = "#0000FF" bgcolor =
"#00FF00">
        <p>Use a different color hexa for the
body and table and see what the result
is.</p>

        <table bgcolor = "#000000">
            <tr>
                <td>
                    <font color = "#FFFFFF">This
text will be shown as white on black
background.</font>
                </td>
            </tr>
        </table>
    </body>

</html>
```

The output is:

Use a different color hexa for the body and table and see what the result is

This text will be shown as white on black background

RGB Values

The rgb() property is used to specify this value, and it will take three values – one red, one for green, and one for blue. That value may be a percentage or an integer from 0 to 255.

Be aware that not all browsers will support this color property, so it isn't really recommended.

These are some of the colors that use the RGB values:

Color	Color RGB
	rgb(0,0,0)
	rgb(255,0,0)
	rgb(0,255,0)
	rgb(0,0,255)

rgb(255,255,0)

rgb(0,255,255)

rgb(255,0,255)

rgb(192,192,192)

rgb(255,255,255)

Here's an example showing how to use the rgb() property to set a tag's background:

```
<!DOCTYPE html>
<html>

    <head>
        <title>HTML Colors by RGB code</title>
    </head>

    <body text = "rgb(0,0,255)" bgcolor =
"rgb(0,255,0)">
        <p>Use a different color code for the
body and table and see what the result
is.</p>

        <table bgcolor = "rgb(0,0,0)">
            <tr>
                <td>
```

```
                  <font color =
    "rgb(255,255,255)">This text will be shown
    as white on a black background.</font>
                  </td>
                </tr>
              </table>
            </body>

        </html>
```

The output is:

Use a different color code for the body and table and see what the result is.

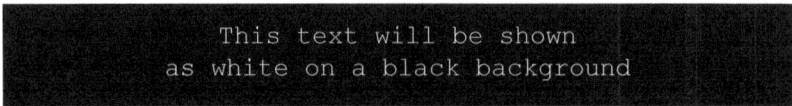

Browser Safe Colors

These colors, 216 of them, are deemed safe and computer-independent. They vary from 000000 to FFFFFF and are supported on all computers that have a minimum 256 color palette.

		000066	000099	0000CC	0000FF
003300	003333	003366	003399	0033CC	0033FF
006600	006633	006666	006699	0066CC	0066FF
009900	009933	009966	009999	0099CC	0099FF

00CC00	00CC33	00CC66	00CC99	00CCCC	00CCFF
00FF00	00FF33	00FF66	00FF99	00FFCC	00FFFF
330000	330033	330066	330099	3300CC	3300FF
333300	333333	333366	333399	3333CC	3333FF
336600	336633	336666	336699	3366CC	3366FF
339900	339933	339966	339999	3399CC	3399FF
33CC00	33CC33	33CC66	33CC99	33CCCC	33CCFF
33FF00	33FF33	33FF66	33FF99	33FFCC	33FFFF
660000	660033	660066	660099	6600CC	6600FF
663300	663333	663366	663399	6633CC	6633FF
666600	666633	666666	666699	6666CC	6666FF
669900	669933	669966	669999	6699CC	6699FF
66CC00	66CC33	66CC66	66CC99	66CCCC	66CCFF
66FF00	66FF33	66FF66	66FF99	66FFCC	66FFFF
990000	990033	990066	990099	9900CC	9900FF
993300	993333	993366	993399	9933CC	9933FF

996600	996633	996666	996699	9966CC	9966FF
999900	999933	999966	999999	9999CC	9999FF
99CC00	99CC33	99CC66	99CC99	99CCCC	99CCFF
99FF00	99FF33	99FF66	99FF99	99FFCC	99FFFF
CC0000	CC0033	CC0066	CC0099	CC00CC	CC00FF
CC3300	CC3333	CC3366	CC3399	CC33CC	CC33FF
CC6600	CC6633	CC6666	CC6699	CC66CC	CC66FF
CC9900	CC9933	CC9966	CC9999	CC99CC	CC99FF
CCCC00	CCCC33	CCCC66	CCCC99	CCCCCC	CCCCFF
CCFF00	CCFF33	CCFF66	CCFF99	CCFFCC	CCFFFF
FF0000	FF0033	FF0066	FF0099	FF00CC	FF00FF
FF3300	FF3333	FF3366	FF3399	FF33CC	FF33FF
FF6600	FF6633	FF6666	FF6699	FF66CC	FF66FF
FF9900	FF9933	FF9966	FF9999	FF99CC	FF99FF
FFCC00	FFCC33	FFCC66	FFCC99	FFCCCC	FFCCFF
FFFF00	FFFF33	FFFF66	FFFF99	FFFFCC	FFFFFF

HTML Fonts

Alongside colors and background images, fonts also play an important role in ensuring your website is user-friendly, and your content is readable. The face and color of the font you use are entirely dependent on the browser and hardware being used to look at the website, but the <font> tag helps us add style, color, and size to the website text. The <basefont> tag is used when you want all your text set as the same size, color, and face.

The <font> tag has a possible three attributes – size, face, and color. If you want to change any of these attributes at any time, all you need to do is use <font> Until the <font tag> has been closed, the text that follows it will stay changed. You can use one <font> tag to change one or all of the attributes.

Setting the Font Size

The <size> attribute is used to set the font size. Accepted values range from 1 right up to 7 but the default is 3.

Here's an example:

```
<!DOCTYPE html>
<html>

    <head>
        <title>Setting Font Size</title>
    </head>

    <body>
        <font size = "1">Font size =
"1"</font><br />
```

```
      <font size = "2">Font size =
"2"</font><br />
      <font size = "3">Font size =
"3"</font><br />
      <font size = "4">Font size =
"4"</font><br />
      <font size = "5">Font size =
"5"</font><br />
      <font size = "6">Font size =
"6"</font><br />
      <font size = "7">Font size =
"7"</font>
   </body>

</html>
```

The output would be:

```
Font size = "1"
Font size = "2"
Font size = "3"
Font size = "4"
Font size = "5"
Font size = "6"
Font size = "7"
```

Relative Font Size

It is also possible to specify the number of sizes larger or smaller than the preset you want the size to be. The syntax would be:

<font size = "+n">

Or

<font size = "−n">

Here's an example:

```
<!DOCTYPE html>
<html>

    <head>
        <title>Relative Font Size</title>
    </head>

    <body>
        <font size = "-1">Font size = "-
1"</font><br />
        <font size = "+1">Font size =
"+1"</font><br />
        <font size = "+2">Font size =
"+2"</font><br />
        <font size = "+3">Font size =
"+3"</font><br />
        <font size = "+4">Font size =
"+4"</font>
    </body>

</html>
```

The output would be:

```
Font size = "-1"
Font size = "+1"
Font size = "+2"
Font size = "+3"
Font size = "+4"
```

Setting the Font Face

The <face> attribute is used to set the font face, but you need to be aware of one thing – if a website user does not have this particular font installed, they cannot see it. Instead, they will be shown the default font that applies to their particular setup.

Here's an example:

```
<!DOCTYPE html>
<html>
    <head>
        <title>Font Face</title>
    </head>

    <body>
        <font face = "Times New Roman" size =
"5">Times New Roman</font><br />
        <font face = "Verdana" size =
"5">Verdana</font><br />
        <font face = "Comic sans MS" size ="
5">Comic Sans MS</font><br />
        <font face = "WildWest" size =
"5">WildWest</font><br />
        <font face = "Bedrock" size =
"5">Bedrock</font><br />
    </body>
</html>
```

The output would be:

Times New Roman

Verdana

Comic Sans MS

WildWest

Bedrock

Specifying Alternate Font Faces

Because the user cannot see your font if they don't have it installed, you can specify more font faces as alternatives. All you do is list each font name with a comma separating them, for example:

```
<font face = "arial,helvetica">
<font face = "Lucida Calligraphy,Comic Sans
MS,Lucida Console">
```

Once your page loads, the user's browser shows the first available font face. If the user does not have any of your specified fonts installed, they will be shown Times New Roman, which is the default.

Setting the Font Color

You can choose whatever font color you want by using the <color> attribute. As discussed earlier in this chapter, you can choose your color using the color name or the color's hexadecimal code.

Here's an example:

```
<!DOCTYPE html>
<html>

   <head>
      <title>Setting Font Color</title>
   </head>

   <body>
      <font color = "#FF00FF">This text is
blue</font><br />
      <font color = "red">This text is
green</font>
```

```
    </body>

    </html>
```

The results would be:

```
This text is in blue
This text is green
```

The <basefont> tag

We can use the <basefont> tag to set the default face, color, and size for all parts of the document that haven't been included in a <font> tag. The <font> tag can be used to override <basefont> settings.

<basefont> will take the three <font> attributes – size, color, and face – and relative font is also supported by providing one of two values, for example, +1 for a one-size larger font or -2 for two sizes smaller.

Here's an example:

```
<!DOCTYPE html>
<html>

    <head>
        <title>Setting Basefont Color</title>
    </head>

    <body>
        <basefont face = "arial, verdana,
sans-serif" size = "2" color = "#ff0000">
        <p>This is the default font.</p>
```

```
     <h2>Example of the &lt;basefont&gt;
Element</h2>

     <p><font size = "+2" color =
"darkpink">
          This is dark pink text with two
sizes larger
       </font>
     </p>

     <p><font face = "courier" size = "-1"
color = "#000000">
          This is courier font, one size
smaller and black.
       </font>
     </p>
  </body>

</html>
```

The result is:

This is the page's default font.

Example of the <basefont> Element

This is dark pink text with two sizes larger

This is courier font, one size smaller and black.

Chapter 14

Creating an HTML Webpage

In our final chapter, we are going to build a basic HTML web page from scratch. Once created, save the page, and then you can see it in your browser. You can also use it to test out different colors, fonts, images, and so on, just to get a better grasp on how it all works and the effects your changes will have.

Start With the Head

Start by opening a text editor. If you use Windows, you can use Notepad/Notepad++ or use TextEdit if you use Mac. Chrome users can make use of Text:

Windows:

1. Open your Start menu

2. Type Notepad or Notepad++ and click on the result as it appears

Mac

1. Click on Spotlight

2. Type textedit and double-click on the result

Chrome OS

1. Open Launcher

2. Click on Text – it may say Code Pad

In your text editor:

1. Type <!DOCTYPE html> and press the enter key – this will let the browser know it is an HTML document

2. Type <html> and press Enter – this provides your code with its opening tag

3. Type <head> and press on Enter. This opens the HTML head. Normally, the head information is now shown on a web page – it can include metadata, title information, scripting languages, CSS style sheets, and more.

4. Next, type <title> - this tag allows you to give your page a title

5. Input your web page title, whatever you want to be shown on the page

6. Follow this with </title> and press Enter, thus providing the closing title tag

7. Type </head> and press on Enter, closing the head. You should know have code like this:

```
<!DOCTYPE html>
<html>
<head>
```

```
<title>My Web Page</title>
</head>
```

Add a Body and Some Text

1. Beneath the closed <head>, type in <body>. The HTML document body is now open, and anything types in this tag will be seen on the page.

2. Type <h1> - this gives your HTML document a heading, which is seen in large text, in bold, and at the top of the document.

3. Type in a page heading – this can be anything, from your page title to a simple greeting.

4. After the heading text, type in </h1> to close the heading tag and press Enter.

From here, you can add whatever headings you want on your page. You can choose from six heading styles, <h1> through <h6>, as demonstrated earlier in the book. As a refresher, you could have three headings of different sizes in succession, such as:

```
<h1>Welcome to this page!</h1>
<h2>My name is Jimmy.</h2>
<h3>I hope you have fun here.</h3>
```

The different headings indicate how important the text is but, even if you don't use an <h1> or <h2> tag, you can still use an <h3> tag – you don't have to use them in order.

5. Now type <p> to open a paragraph – this is where text will be displayed in normal sizes.

6. Type in your text – perhaps a web page description or some other information you want your users to see

7. Once you have typed in your text, type </p> to close the tag and press enter. Your paragraph text could look like this:

```
<p> This is my first paragraph</>
```

Again, additional paragraphs can be added in the same way, and multiple <p> tags can be used in a row if you want multiple paragraphs shown under a single heading.

The text color can also be changed by using <font color="color> and the </font> tags to frame the text. Ensure that you type in the color you want in the "color" part, inside the quote marks. Using these tags, you can change the color of any of your text. For example, if you wanted to change one paragraph into red text, you would type the following:

```
<p><font color="red">(your text
here)</font></p>
```

You can also add other formats, such as italics, bold, and so on. Here are some examples:

```
<b>Bold text</b>
<i>Italic text</i>
<u>Underlined text</u>
<sub>Subscript text</sub>
<sup>Superscript text</sup>
```

If you want to use italics and bold to emphasize text, rather than just for styling, use <em> and <strong> rather than <i> and <b>. This will ensure your web page can be understood easier when screen readers or other assistive technologies are used.

Add Some More Elements

There are various elements that you can add:

Adding a picture

1. Open an image tag by typing <img src =

2. Paste or type in the image URL straight after the = and then close your image tag with >

For example, if you are using something like http://wwwmyimage.com/mountains, you would type in this:

```
<img
src="http://www.myimage.com/mountains.jpg">
```

Linking to a different page

1. Open a link tag by typing <a href=

2. Paste or type the link URL straight after the =

3. Type > to close the link

4. After the >, type the link name

5. Follow this with </a>

For example, if you wanted to link to Wikipedia, it would look like this:

```
<a
href="https://www.wikipedia.com">Wikipedia</
a>.
```

Adding a line break

To add line breaks, simply type <br> where you want it. A horizontal line is created, dividing your page into sections.

Customize Your Colors

First, decide what colors you want and where and pick your color names or the hexadecimal code that relates to it, or you can use the decimal value, although this isn't recommended.

Next, we want to change the background color, and this is done using the <body> tag with the style attribute. For example, you could change the background color to lilac, like this:

```
<body style="background-color:lilac;">
```

Now, we want to set the color of the text for any of the tags. This can also be done using the style attribute, allowing you to specify what color you want the text to be in any specific tag. For example, you might want to make the text in a <p> tag dark blue:

```
<p style="color:darkblue;">
```

This change will only be effected on the text in the specified <p> tag. If you started another <p> tag later on, and you also want the text in that to be darkblue, you would need to include the style attribute.

Setting the Header or Paragraph Background Color

This is done in much the same way as the <body> tag. Let's assume that you want one of your <p> tags to have a lightblue background, while an <h1> tag should have a background of lilac. Here's what you would do:

```
<p style="background-color:lightblue;">
<h1 style="background-color:lilac;">
```

Close Your Document

To close the body, type </body>. This should be added once all your text and other elements like links and images are added. This tag will tell the browser not to expect any more code.

To close an HTML document, type </html> after the HTML body. This will tell the browser not to expect any more HTML code.

Now, your whole document should look something like this, depending, of course, on what details you included:

```
<!DOCTYPE html>
<html>

<head>
<title>Wikipedia Home Page</title>
</head>

<body>

<h1>Welcome to My Page!</h1>
<p>This is the home page for Wikipedia. Come
in and enjoy!</p>
```

```
<h2>Important Dates</h2>
<p><i>January 15, 2021</i> - Wikipedia's
20th Birthday</p>

<h2>Links</h2>
<p>Here is a link to wikipedia: <a
href="http://www.wikipedia.com">wikipedia</a
></p>

</body>
</html>
```

Save Your Web Page and Open it

Mac users must first convert their document into plain text. To do this, click on Format at the top of your screen and choose Make Plain Text from the drop-down menu. You do NOT need to do this on Windows; indeed, you can't – there is no facility to do so.

1. All users should click File on the top menu

2. Click on Save As from the dropdown menu

Alternatively, on Windows, you can press on CTRL+S and, on Mac, you can press ⌘ Command+S.

3. Name your HTML document – it doesn't matter what it is, so long as you remember it. This is done in the File Name box in Windows and the Name box in Mac.

4. Next, the document type must be changed to HTML. On Windows, click on Save As>All Files and add .html to the

end of the file name. On macOS, add .txt to the end of the file name. Click on Save, and the file is created.

5. Now you can close your text editor so the file can be opened and viewed in your browser.

6. Opening your file in a browser is as simple as double-clicking on it. If that doesn't work, Windows users should right-click the document and click on Open With (your browser). Mac users should single-click on the document and then click File>Open With (your browser)

The last step is to make any edits to your document that you want. For example, you may spot an error on your page that needs fixing and, to do this, the document text must be edited:

1. Windows users – right-click on the document and click on Edit in the drop-down menu. If you are using Notepad++ as your text editor, this option will read "Edit with Notepad++."

2. Mac users should click on the document once, then click on File>Open With>TextEdit. Alternatively, the file can be dragged into TextEdit

3. Chromebook users should close Text (the text editor app), and click on Files, then click on your file.

And that brings us to the end. This should give you the basics you need to create whatever style of web page you want.

HTML Tag References

This provides you with a quick guide to all the HTML tags you need:

Basic HTML

Tag	Description
<!DOCTYPE>	Used for defining the type of document
<html>	Used for defining HTML documents
<head>	Used to hold information or metadata about your document
<title>	Used for defining the document's title
<body>	Used for defining the body of the document
<h1> to <h6>	Used for defining the different headings
<p>	Used for defining paragraphs
 	Used for defining a line break
<hr>	Used for defining changes to the document theme
<!--...-->	Used for defining comments

HTML Formatting

Tag	Description
\<acronym>	Used for defining acronyms – this is NOT supported in HTML5 - \<abbr> should be used instead
\<abbr>	Used for defining acronyms or abbreviations
\<address>	Used for defining content owner or author contact information
\<b>	Used for defining text in bold
\<bdi>	Used for isolating a section of text that may have different direction formatting to the text surrounding it
\<bdo>	Used for overriding the current direction for the text
\<big>	Used for defining big text – this is NOT supported in HTML5 – CSS should be used instead
\<blockquote>	Used for defining a quote that comes from a different source
\<center>	Used for defining centered text – this is NOT supported in HTML5 - CSS should be used instead
\<cite>	Used for defining a work's title

<code>	Used for defining computer code
<del>	Used for defining deleted text
<dfn>	Used for specifying terms that will be defined in the page content
<em>	Used for defining text that is emphasized in some way
<font>	Used for defining the color, font, and size of the text – this NOT supported in HTML5 – CSS should be used instead
<i>	Used for defining text in an alternative mood or voice
<ins>	Used for defining text inserted into the document
<kbd>	Used for defining specific keyboard input
<mark>	Used for defining marked or highlighted text
<meter>	Used for defining scalar measures within a gauge or a known range
<pre>	Use for defining preformatted text
<progress>	Used for representing a task's progress
<q>	Used for defining short quotations
<rp>	Used for defining what is shown in

	browsers that do not require any Ruby annotations
\<rt\>	Used for defining incorrect text
\<ruby\>	Used for defining ruby annotations – used in East Asian typography
\<s\>	Used for defining incorrect text
\<samp\>	Used for defining computer program sample outputs
\<small\>	Used for defining smaller text
\<strike\>	Used for defining strikethrough text – this is NOT supported in HTML5 – use \<s\> or \<del\> instead
\<strong\>	Used for defining important text
\<sub\>	Used for defining subscripted text
\<sup\>	Used for defining superscripted text
\<template\>	Used for defining containers to hold text that should not be seen on the loading page
\<time\>	Used for defining specific dates or datetimes
\<tt\>	Used for defining teletype text – this is NOT supported n HTML5 – CSS should be used instead

Tag	
<u>	Used of defining unarticulated text that has a different style to normal text
<var>	Used for defining variables
<wbr>	Used for defining possible line breaks

Forms and Input

Tag	Description
<button>	Used for defining a clickable button
<datalist>	Used for specifying pre-defined option lists for input controls
<fieldset>	Used to group related elements together in a form
<form>	Used for defining HTML forms for user input
<input>	Used for defining input controls
<label>	Used for defining <input> element labels
<legend>	Used for defining <fieldset> element captions
<optgroup>	Used for defining related groups of items in drop-down lists
<option>	Used for defining one option in a drop-down list

<output>	Used for defining a calculation's result
<select>	Used for defining drop-down lists
<textarea>	Used for defining input controls with multiple lines – text areas

Frames

Tag	Description
<frame>	Used for defining frames or windows in framesets – NOT supported in HTML5
<frameset>	Used for defining sets of frames – NOT supported in HTML5
<noframes>	Used for defining alternative content where users' computers/browsers do not support frames – NOT supported in HTML5
<iframe>	Used for defining inline frames

Images

Tag	Description
<area>	Used for defining areas inside image maps
<canvas>	Used for drawing graphics via scripting

	– on the fly, typically using JavaScript
\<figcaption>	Used for defining a \<figure> element's caption
\<figure>	Used for specifying content that is self-contained
\<img>	Used for defining images
\<map>	Used for defining image maps on the client-side
\<picture>	Used for defining containers to hold multiple resources for images
\<svg>	Used for defining an SVG graphics container

Audio / Video

Tag	Description
\<audio>	Used for defining sound content
\<source>	Used for defining several media resources, such as \<video>, \<picture>, and \<audio>
\<track>	Used for defining media element text tracks - \<video> and \<audio>
\<video>	Used for defining movies or videos

287

Links

Tag	Description
<a>	Used for defining hyperlinks
<link>	Used for defining relationships between documents and external resources – typically used when linking to a style sheet
<nav>	Used for defining navigation links

Lists

Tag	Description
<dd>	Used for defining descriptions of names or terms in description lists
<dir>	Used for defining directory lists – this is NOT supported in HTML5 – <ul> should be used instead
<dl>	Used for defining description lists
<dt>	Used for defining names or terms in description lists
<li>	Used for defining list items
<ol>	Used for defining ordered lists
<ul>	Used for defining unordered lists

Tables

Tag	Description
<table>	Used for defining tables
<caption>	Used for defining captions on tables
<th>	Used for defining header cells in tables
<tr>	Used for defining rows in tables
<td>	Used for defining cells in tables
<thead>	Used for grouping a table's header content
<tbody>	Used for grouping a table's body content
<tfoot>	Used for grouping a table's footer content
<col>	Used for specifying the properties for each column in <colgroup>
<colgroup>	Used for specifying one or more columns grouped in a table to be formatted

Styles and Semantics

Tag	Description
\<article>	Used for defining articles
\<aside>	Used for defining a document's content that isn't page content
\<data>	Used for adding machine-readable translations of specified content
\<details>	Used for defining extra details that can be hidden or viewed by the user
\<dialog>	Used for defining dialog windows or boxes
\<div>	Used for defining sections in documents
\<footer>	Used for defining a section or document's footer
\<header>	Used for defining a section or document's header
\<main>	Used for specifying a document's main content
\<section>	Used for defining a document's sections

<span>	Used for defining sections in documents
<style>	Used for defining a document's style information
<summary>	Used for defining a <details> tag's visible headings

Meta Info

Tag	Description
<base>	Used for specifying a base target or URL for all a document's relative URLs
<basefont>	Used for specifying default size, color, and font for all document text – this is NOT supported in HTML5 – CSS should be used instead
<head>	Used for defining specific information about the document
<meta>	Used for defining the document's metadata

Programming

Tag	Description

\<applet>	Used for defining embedded applets – this is NOT supported in HTML5 - \<object> or \<embed> should be used instead
\<embed>	Used for defining containers to hold no-HTML (external) applications
\<noscript>	Used for defining alternative content where a user's setup doesn't support client-side scripts
\<object>	Used for defining embedded objects
\<param>	Used for defining an object's parameters
\<script>	Used for defining client-side scripts

Conclusion

Thank you for taking the time to read my guide. If you made it to the end, you should have a certain level of comfort using HTML and understand how it lets content creators and developers create and build their web pages.

HTML is a far bigger subject than this book but what I have covered are the basics. You now know what HTML is, what it is made up of, and how to use the most common elements, tags, and attributes. You learned, in short, how to build a basic webpage using only HTML.

As with any programming language, the only way to get truly comfortable with using HTML is to use it – the more you practice, the more familiar you will become with it. That practice includes trying to build your own web pages and going into other people's HTML code and trying to understand how it has been used and what it has done.

Be patient. No language is easy to learn, and there will be many bumps in the road. Don't beat yourself up if you make mistakes. Learn from them and put right where you went wrong, and constantly try to improve and push yourself just that little bit harder.

Take the time out to think about elements and use the class and id attributes to identify the important one. This is important in learning how best to organize the structure of your documents.

There are plenty of online resources and courses in HTML available; use them and build your knowledge layer by layer.

References

"HTML - Basic Tags - Tutorialspoint." *Tutorialspoint.com*, 2019, www.tutorialspoint.com/html/html_basic_tags.htm.

"HTML Tutorial." *W3schools.com*, 2018, www.w3schools.com/html/.

Schäferhoff, Nick. "HTML Tutorial for Beginners 101 (Including HTML5 Tags) WebsiteSetup." *Websitesetup.org*, 8 May 2019, websitesetup.org/html-tutorial-beginners/.

"Structuring the Web with HTML - Learn Web Development | MDN." *Developer.mozilla.org*, developer.mozilla.org/en-US/docs/Learn/HTML. Accessed 19 Mar. 2021.

"Tutorials - Javatpoint." *Www.javatpoint.com*, 2011, www.javatpoint.com/.

www.ingramcontent.com/pod-product-compliance
Lightning Source LLC
Chambersburg PA
CBHW071331210326
41597CB00015B/1415